Hollywood
LESBIANS

Hollywood

L E S B I A N S

Conversations With:

SANDY DENNIS

BARBARA STANWYCK

MARJORIE MAIN

NANCY KULP

PATSY KELLY

AGNES MOOREHEAD

EDITH HEAD

DOROTHY ARZNER

CAPUCINE

JUDITH ANDERSON

by Boze Hadleigh

BARRICADE BOOKS / NEW YORK

Published by Barricade Books Inc.
61 Fourth Avenue
New York, NY 10003

Printed in the United States of America.

Library of Congress Cataloging-in-Publication Data

Hadleigh, Boze.
    Hollywood lesbians / Boze Hadleigh.
        p.   cm.
    ISBN 1-56980-014-6: $21.95
    1. Lesbian actresses — United States — Interviews. 2. Motion
picture actors and actresses — United States — Interviews. I. Title.
PN1995.9.L48H23   1994
791.43'028'092273 — dc20   94-25584
                                                   CIP

Designed by Cindy LaBreacht
First printing

AND ALWAYS FOR RONNIE

The Films of Jane Fonda

Conversations With My Elders

Hispanic Hollywood

The Vinyl Closet

Leading Ladies (UK)

The Lavender Screen

Hollywood, Babble On

CONTENTS

ACKNOWLEDGMENTS

WITH WARM THANKS to those mentioned in this book, and to: Noelle Azzopardi, Ruth Bachelor, Dorothy Denny, Joyce Haber, Susan Hayward, Stan Kamen, Neil Koenigsberg, Anita Loos, Dorothy Manners, Stan Musgrove, Cesar Romero, Sam Steward, Jane Wagner, and Aida Zieff.

For photos from their collections, Rae Burke, Rose Hellman, Helen Livingston, and Naomi Walders.

For their insight and empowerment of this project, Lyle and Carole Stuart.

And of course, Linda Fresia.

INTRODUCTION

For three years in the early 1980s, I edited the newsletter of our San Mateo County chapter of NOW. Monica, a lesbian classmate from the University of California, Santa Barbara, remained a close friend and had urged me to join the National Organization for Women (famous male members included Phil Donahue and Alan Alda).

I already subscribed to *Ms.* magazine and had contributed money to this underrated cause—the rights and dignity of more than half the human race. But Monica encouraged me to become visibly affiliated. "It's important for them in smaller towns to see that men also care." Most of our NOW meetings drew a dozen or so participants, never more than two guys.

If sometimes I felt conspicuous or like a third wheel, I knew I was doing my valuable bit once I became editor. After the first year I would gladly have stepped aside, but no other member felt she or he had the requisite time or skills for producing an informative, exhortative newsletter that reached more than fifteen hundred homes. (I often wondered, if that many locals were interested enough to join, why didn't more than twelve or fifteen ever show up at a time?) So I stayed on as editor, with estimable assistance, for two more terms.

A few years later, I published a collection of interviews with gay men of film (a designer, two actors, three directors). *Conversations With My Elders*—not my chosen title—was eagerly received here and abroad, a first-of-its-kind volume that eventually became a "cult" book. Monica was the first woman to write to me about it, from Australia. Her rave preceded a question that she would repeat annually: "When are you going to do a book on Hollywood Lesbians?"

I replied that it was only a matter of time until such an interesting and overdue project materialized, and that I imagined it would be done by a female. I'd already interviewed some "lavender ladies", as Patsy Kelly called them, among them Kelly, Marjorie Main, Agnes Moorehead, and reclusive lesbian legend Dorothy Arzner.

I also continued to interview, usually on assignment, heterosexual stars and gay and lesbian ones allergic to or scared of the truth. Such sessions typically revolved around soundbites about the celebrities' opposite-sex "dates" or for-show contractual mates. But then, magazine and newspaper editors also had an aversion to questions about sexual and affectional orientation, even when—so very rarely—they were willingly and honestly answered.

One day a Manhattan editor asked about a possible interview with "any beautiful French actress," to counter the competition's recent one with Catherine Deneuve.

I suggested Capucine, who'd just completed a sequel to her sixties hit, *The Pink Panther.*

"Perfect!"

I stated that Capucine was reportedly lesbian and being European and no longer a leading lady, might assent to discuss her private life.

"Oh, no!" He wanted the interview "light and accessible" to average readers. Then he had her researched and said I must mention that she'd changed her name from Germaine — "which is common as mud in French" — to Capucine, *nasturtium*, "her favorite flower." And I should stress — "the ladies'll love this!" — that in her Hollywood debut, playing a princess, Capucine had worn forty gowns with 21,000 yards of material. And she'd won the coveted role over 100 other "girls."

Fortunately, she declined the interview.

I later interviewed Capucine on our own terms. I'd sent her a copy of my book, *Conversations With My Elders,* and she agreed to speak with me partly because I spoke French and had interviewed George Cukor and Rock Hudson. She admitted she hadn't read the entire book because it's harder in a foreign language. Likewise, I sent copies to Nancy Kulp and Sandy Dennis, who both relished it, and Barbara Stanwyck, who had "reservations," and Judith Anderson, who consented to an interview "despite such an open book."

So, finally, Monica, here's that book. Someone had to do it, and it was a pleasure and a privilege. Like you, I feel it's a bit of herstory, valuable Hollywood herstory too often ignored or suppressed. This interview collection of lesbian and bi women of film (two nonthespians, three comedic actors, five dramatic actresses) spans the 1970s to the nineties. The women vary in every conceivable way, from time, place, and humor to self-image, openness and raised consciousness.

I am hopeful that this book offers more than a glimpse inside the tinsel closet, that it is an up-front look at the public and private lives of ten fascinating and accomplished women. My book is dedicated to their enduring spirit and to you, Monica.

March 11, 1994
Beverly Hills, California

Funny Ladies

MARJORIE MAIN

(1 8 9 0 – 1 9 7 5)

For three decades, all of America knew Marjorie Main's face. And her voice. The latter was often described as resembling a crow's. The face was prettyish, but the "sack-of-taters figure" and the "messy nest of hair" had all the glamour of, well, Ma Kettle, whom she first enacted in 1947, to Oscar-nominated acclaim. Before that, Main had played umpteen mothers on stage (even to Mae West, two years her junior) and screen (Humphrey Bogart, Barbara Stanwyck, etc.)

She was born Mary Tomlinson but felt compelled to change her name when she took up acting, a profession detested by her minister father. Damon Runyon would later write, "It's difficult to reconcile the name Marjorie with Marjorie Main's appearance and her manner. She has a dead pan, square shoulders, a stocky build, a voice like a file, and an uncurried aspect. She has a stride like a section boss."

"Battle-ax" was another frequently used description of the highly successful character actress who was invariably cast as a mother and/or in comedic roles. She didn't find her niche until middle age, progressing from a stock company to vaudeville to Broadway and movies—landing a contract at MGM and then starring in the low-brow but highly profitable Ma and Pa Kettle series which helped see Universal through the turbulent 1950s, when television was taking its toll on all movie studios.

Along the way, Main—whose mothering was limited to the screen—engaged in a belated marriage to a psychologist about a quarter-century her senior. They worked together via his lecture tours, and certain insiders felt it was a passionless merger. Main temporarily gave up the stage, but returned—possibly against the wishes of her husband, Dr. Krebs, who died at seventy-one in 1935. By then, Main had made her screen bow, initially stereotyped as "dramatic slum mother" after making her mark as Bogey's mom in the hit, *Dead End* (1937). The same year, she provided maternal support in the hit, *Stella Dallas*.

In 1940, Marjorie was cast as Mehitabel, a blacksmith, opposite the even gruffer Wallace Beery, in *Wyoming*. She was seventh-billed but stole the show and accepted a seven-year contract from Louis B. Mayer. Between 1940 and 1954, she was one of MGM's most popular stock players, no longer limited to the slums but still a harridan and eventually typed as a rural gal thanks to her farmer and hillbilly impersonations.

Mayer costarred Main in remakes of films that had starred another mannish comedienne, the late Marie Dressler. Marjorie was Beery's match in gumption and sass, and at age fifty began a new phase of her career. But despite six movies together, she couldn't stand the crude and boozy Beery (also notorious for his penchant for young girls). Her free-wheeling image notwithstanding, Main was a firm believer in no drinking and no smoking. Even during her career, she was a private, home-bound woman. She didn't undertake publicity or mix much with fellow actors. Her private circle was small and numbered a few unwed or long-divorced non-actresses. One of her few show biz pals was Spring Byington, another once-wed but non-man-oriented thespian.

Most of Main's final films featured Ma Kettle, the kindly but iron-willed mother of thirteen or more. Main got along fine with Percy Kilbride, the soft-spoken lifelong bachelor who played Pa Kettle for most of the series until a contractual dispute. In 1957 Marjorie Main bade farewell to the movies and tried a few guest shots on episodic television, which she found too fast-paced for her liking.

Her retirement took, and until 1975, she never looked back at the roles she might have had. Because she'd invested wisely, she was able to live in style in Hollywood and Palm Springs, without any need for work and with little desire for publicity. In the early 1970s, having recently discovered the Kettle movies on TV, I made inquiries about interviewing Ms. Main for one of the then-numerous movie magazines I wrote for. I was told she was a near-recluse who shunned the public.

But in 1973, I saw her riding merrily in the annual Hollywood Santa Claus Lane parade, basking in the public's recognition and applause. I found out that she rode in the parade every year and was particularly fond of her younger fans. (I'd earlier read a quote in which she explained—facetiously?—that her dislike for babies was due to their lack of profile.)

I got a green-light from *Modern Screen*, the top movie magazine at the time, for a nostalgia-ridden interview with "Marjorie 'Ma Kettle' Main, Hollywood's Most Determined Mother!!" But I couldn't find a show business contact through whom to approach her. Just after turning twenty in 1974, I discovered that the ex-actress had been a good friend of the late sister of one of my mother's PTA friends. I obtained her phone number, and we agreed to meet at the Hollywood Hills home of the PTA woman who had moved there from Santa Barbara.

Once the session was set—over tea and cookies—I decided that it would be more interesting to have an open-ended conversation with Marjorie Main than a formal and now-tell-me-about-*that*-movie interview. If our chat went well, then we could meet later, perhaps at her own home, for the *Modern Screen*-tailored interview. My own questions and curiosity didn't dovetail with those of the average *M.S.* reader.

Especially as I'd long since heard from associates that Main had been "very close" to Spring Byington, who by all accounts was actively lesbian. When I first heard that, it hadn't immediately occurred to me that Marjorie might herself be equally non-heterosexual. For some time, I could hardly believe it of Miss Byington, who died in 1971 after decades of fame as the genteel, feminine-voiced mother of everyone from Jo, Meg, Beth, and Amy to Ronald Reagan on the big and little screen. When one is young, one believes devoutly in stereotypes.

On Cordell Drive—the same street on which *Little Women* director George Cukor lived—I met the well-dressed, cordial, and laughing-eyed Ms. Main. Nor did her raucous voice disappoint. She was like Ma Kettle's older, city-bred sister, and charming. Our hostess, delighted to have a celebrity in her house, joined us long enough to pour the first cup, then shyly summoned her housekeeper, asking her to please see to our needs—via a tinkling silver bell on the tea table—whilst she went shopping.

From the start, Majorie Main was affable yet firm about what she would and wouldn't discuss ("Let's avoid questions about Mr. Mayer," she said cryptically). However, when the afternoon ended, I was surprised by how much she'd revealed in spite of backing away from names and declarations. Shortly before we took our leave with a handshake and a hug, the octogenarian, who hadn't used the word, giggled that it had been "a very gay afternoon, hasn't it?" Then she winked conspiratorially.

The following year while in San Jose working toward my master's degree, I belatedly learned that the big-screen veteran had died earlier in 1975 of cancer. I looked up her obituaries. One stated, "She was among Hollywood's most iconoclastic performers, and one of its most cherished among her peers and the public, having shone in myriad films either popular or acclaimed, or both."

Another obit editorialized its surprise that the woman had "lived alone for the last 40 years" and had never borne children, contrary to her screen image as a "formidable but mush-hearted mother." But, as Main herself put it, they do call it acting.

BH: You began practically at the top. Wasn't your first film directed by William Wyler?

MM: Hold on. To begin with, I'm not sure it [*A House Divided*, 1932] was my first—the first one I made or the first one released. Second, he wasn't *the* William Wyler then. He was just a director, William Wyler. Anyway, who wants to begin at the top? It means there's no place else to go but down! [Laughs.]

BH: You were also in a movie [in 1932] called *Hot Saturday*, with Cary Grant and Randolph Scott, who were then roommates, at least.....

MM: That's right. Tell me the names of the people in 'em—I don't always remember the titles. I did so many!

BH: Here are a few titles. *Women Without Names. There Goes My Heart. The Affairs of Martha. Jackass Mail.* The latter spelled m-a-i-l. Do any ring a bell?

MM: I don't think any of those was big hits! [Smiles.] Not like *Ma and Pa Ketttle at Waikiki.* [Winks.] I retired after that last Kettle picture. I could see the handwriting on the wall. It said *The Kettles on Old MacDonald's Farm.* That was the name of the [last] picture!

BH: **Did the series begin to sink when Percy Kilbride left?**

MM: It didn't help none! We were a team, and when you're a team, you go through with it. [Shakes head.] But that wasn't the whole story. I think they just ran out of stories, plum ran out of imagination. That's always gonna happen with any movie series.

BH: **Did you and Percy get along?**

MM: Like a house on fire. He was a quiet type. He didn't do anywhere near the number of pictures I did, and the more you do, the tougher your hide. He was a sweet soul.

BH: **Percy Kilbride never wed. What do you think his private romantic situation was?**

MM: Dunno. [Glares.] Not for print. I don't talk about men. Men don't talk about ladies, and I don't talk about gentlemen. Percy was a gent.

BH: **His death via a traffic accident was both tragic and ironic, in that he didn't drive. [Kilbride and an actor friend were crossing the street near Percy's Hollywood apartment; both were hit—the friend died instantly, Kilbride eight days later at age seventy-six, in 1964.]**

MM: Automobiles is a curse of sorts....That was one of the saddest days of my life, when I found out he was hit, and then when he passed on. Let's leave it.

BH: **As for Ma and Pa Kettle, Ma usually wore the pants in the family.**

MM: [Laughs.] Between you and me and the world, Ma Kettle was the real man in the family!

BH: **In many ways she was ahead of her time. Except of course for having so many children.**

MM: It was all a joke. The idea that little old Pa could have sired so many kids, and then whenever Ma got bumptious and played the dominant character, all that made audiences laugh. They didn't take none of it seriously.

BH: **I think that you're more associated with housework than any other actress in motion pictures.**

MM: You may be right! I usually played gals who were deep into housework. Personally, I think housework stinks! Dusting's the worst—so pointless. But I do it. Housework's good for you, and it's discipline.

BH: **You retired so long ago. Haven't you missed acting? Especially since, toward the end, you starred in your own movies?**

MM: Yeah, I kinda liked the fuss. But I did enough acting to last me....'Course I miss it, now and then. But I just wait a while and the mood passes.

BH: **Do you still get offers?**

MM: You mean for work? [Winks, laughs.] Some.

BH: **What sort of roles are you offered? More Ma Kettles?**

MM: That's partly why I don't get many offers—everything's gone away from the farms. The country's gone urban-suburban, it's all about cities now, all the pictures, the TV shows. They don't make stories about farms and farmers now, 'cause less people farm.

BH: **Farmers are underrepresented.**

MM: 'Course they are! Even if there's fewer of 'em, they're still the backbone of this country. And they love to see stories about their own. All the farmers went to all of the Ma and Pa Kettle pictures, they were loyal.

BH: Wasn't there a downside to being associated with farm roles?

MM: 'Course there was. Nowadays, the only offers I don't get is refined types. Ladies. Nobody knows I'm a lady in real life, they think I'm just Ma Kettle, only older and older.

BH: No disrespect to your talent, but I couldn't see you playing a European.

MM: In some quarters, that could be taken as a compliment. I don't mind. I always got picked for my type. I always seemed like somebody's mother.

BH: It's ironic, then, that you never had children.

MM: I s'ppose. [Indifferently.]

BH: But many people expect you to have children, because of your roles?

MM: I was an actress, that's what I played. They do call it acting—at least, they did then!

BH: And one of the most touching mother-love performances on screen was Greta Garbo opposite Freddie Bartholomew in *Anna Karenina*. Garbo, of course, had no children or husband, etc....

MM: I getcha. [Winks.]

BH: You definitely were stereotyped.

MM: If I hadn't been stereotyped, I wouldn't have worked. I wasn't hired for my beauty or my girlish figure. [Giggles.] I played mothers. Only, they wasn't all farm gals or hillbillies.

BH: No. I remember you in *Heaven Can Wait* [1943]. You were Gene Tierney's mother and lived in a mansion. And you had a big fat husband [Eugene Pallette].

MM: I've had husbands of every description, enough to last me a lifetime! Kids, too—usually a whole passel of 'em! [Rolls her eyes.] By gum!

BH: May I ask when your husband died?

MM: My real one? Dr. Krebs died in 1935.

BH: Was there ever any temptation to remarry, since?

MM: Are you kidding? [Laughs.]

BH: I believe I once read a quote where you said you didn't care much for babies because they have no profile?

MM: Sounds like me. Look, Ma Kettle had thirteen kids—at least I think she did, back in *The Egg and I* [1947]. They may have added a few, later on. Anyhow, *that's* acting!

BH: It's a shame few people remember you were nominated for an Academy Award as Ma for *The Egg and I*. Who won Best Supporting Actress in that competition?

MM: [Sourly.] Celestial...Celeste Holm. For *Gentleman's Agreement.*

BH: That semi-daring movie about anti-Semitism whose moral was, don't treat a Jew badly, because he might turn out to be a Christian in disguise.

MM: [Laughs.] I never looked at it that way!

BH: What was Claudette [*Egg*] Colbert like to work with?

MM: She was very grand.

BH: Very grand?

MM: Very.

BH: Grand?

MM: She thought so.

BH: I read in a book called *Hollywood Babylon* that she had an alleged affair with Marlene Dietrich....

MM: Really? A book?! [Smiles] Could be.

BH: Did you ever hear in Hollywood of her off-screen life?

MM: Yep...she had a husband or two. No kids.

BH: When a woman has no children, what does that indicate to you?

MM: She's smart! She can live her own life and not spend it worrying about some ingrate. No one ever tells me they envy me, not having kids, but believe me, some do.

BH: **I read a quote where you were asked about being, as they put it, childless. You said that you regretted it.**

MM: It were long ago. A gal gets asked those questions, and that's the reply they expect,

BH: **Male actors are never asked why they're not fathers.**

MM: With them, it's just "carefree." With an actress, or any female, it's a shame.

BH: **Quote-unquote....I can picture you as a pioneer woman, yet you didn't do many westerns.**

MM: I did a "Wagon Train" for the television. In 1958.

BH: **So you didn't retire in 1957?**

MM: I did. From the movies. But I thought I'd give television a try. By then, we all knew it was here to stay. So I guested on my friend Spring Byington's show, and next year I did the western. I didn't like the pace. Too fast. I was gettin' older, I didn't want to speed up. I wanted to slow down. So I said that's it. Arrivederci.

BH: **Which means "see you later."**

MM: Well, then, adios. That's Spanish, ain't it?

BH: **Si—which is also Italian.**

MM: You got the right pronunciation!

BH: **Of "si"?**

MM: No, Eye-talian! [Laughs.]

BH: **...Spring Byington—was the program "December Bride?"**

MM: You watched it? [Surprised.]

BH: **Oh, I'm older than I look. I loved "December Bride" and the music and the cast.**

MM: It was a real big success for Spring. CBS didn't want her, you know, they thought she was too old. Desi Arnaz just put his foot down, and the stubborn fools had to give in. After all those years [in support], she got to be the star for a change.

BH: I read in a movie source book that Ms. Byington wed once, had no children—of course we remember her as Marmee in *Little Women* [1933]—and was rumored not to be...fond of men, that way....

MM: [Stunned pause, then amusement.] They're saying these things in books now? [Shakes her head.] Spring would roll over in her grave, bless her. It's true, she didn't have much use for men. But she was my friend, and I'll just hold off talking about her private life.

BH: But what can it hurt now? There was nothing wrong with it anyway.

MM: I know. But not everyone's as liberal as you.

BH: You know the other source about her interest in women? George Cukor, who directed that version of *Little Women* with Katharine Hepburn [as Jo].

MM: What's he said about Kate Hepburn?

BH: Virtually nothing revealing, so far. People of that generation seem to think it's an untouchable subject. Their attitude helps make it so.

MM: That'll die out, it's bound to. It's bound to improve, but I can comprehend that if somebody's alive and active, then it's something you don't fool with. Nobody should have his career chances snatched away from him.

BH: Nobody should have her identity or love life taken from her, or have to live a lie.

MM: Unless she becomes an actress! [Laughs.]

BH: An actress....Did you ever feel pressured to get a male escort whenever you wanted to go out on the town?

MM: Never much liked going out on the town. If I'd looked like one of them glamour gals, maybe. I doubt it, though. I liked keeping to myself. I like people, but when I'm not working, I like being on my own. Even then.

BH: Now that you're not working, do you miss people much?

MM: I'm not lonely, but I take comfort in my faith, and it keeps me company.

BH: Can you explain your beliefs?

MM: Not much I can explain, it's a whole other plane. My father was a minister, and I still believe most of those things, but I found it a little too earthbound for my liking. Too many do's and don'ts, and not enough about spirituality.

BH: You're a Spiritualist?

MM: Yes, and I wasn't introduced to it by Mae West, either. Mae's a friend of mine. We worked together in New York [on stage in *The Wicked Age* in 1927], and I visit her up at the Ravenswood [apartment house]. But I'm pretty sure I came to Spiritualism before she did, even though I had one of the shocks of my life when I was minding my own business, reading a magazine, and there was this long article about Mae, and a whole section about her spiritual beliefs, with a list of the people she supposedly converted to the occult and whatnot. My name was on that list! I wrote to the editor and gave him a piece of my mind! Nobody ever introduced me to nothin'!

BH: You explored various religions or sects on your own?

MM: I think it's the sensible thing to do. I made a reading about religion, and I also took to Moral Re-Armament. That used to be a real big movement. I don't smoke or drink, and I never have. I hope you don't?

BH: My mother doesn't drink, nor did her father, who was an army general. Mostly, I don't like the taste. And I might smoke two or three cigarettes a week, at a restaurant, not at home.

MM: That's a start. The worst thing of all now is drugs. It was bad enough with smoking and drinking, but now with drugs, it's all going downhill fast. [Shakes head.]

BH: **May I ask what you played opposite Mae West?**

MM: What else? Her mother! [Laughs.]

BH: **But you're what, only a couple of years older than her?**

MM: I reckon. But she always played younger'n what she was, and I played older.

BH: **It's hard to imagine Mae West having many female friends.**

MM: She's got a few, and she keeps 'em a long time, too. She likes talking with her lady friends. With the gents, she flirts. She's got a good mind, Mae.

BH: **Did you never go out on the town when you were acting?**

MM: I wouldn't say never. I'd go visit friends, but I wasn't much for nightclubs or premieres. That was for the younger set. Dancing and such. There was a lot more nightclubs then. I did go to the Trocadero right after the war; friends arranged it for me, on account of Arthur Blake did an imitation of me. He was pretty good, too!

BH: **You were flattered to be imitated?**

MM: 'Course I was. Arthur Blake was kinda famous himself. Back about that time, it made the papers when Mrs. Roosevelt asked him to quit [imitating her]. So instead he did Mrs. Truman! And lots of stars besides — Bankhead and Carmen Miranda, Gloria Swanson. A real talented gentleman.

BH: **One doesn't—excuse me—associate you with glamour, but I'll bet that you miss the glamour of Hollywood's heyday?**

MM: Not really. Wasn't a part of it. But I miss the decency. Actors at least kept their boozing and chemicals to themselves then, kept it a secret.

BH: **What about the way stars dressed?**

MM: They dressed special...for the public's sake, too! Now, you can tell that the younger stars don't care so much about their public as they do about their salaries or staying home and throwing wild parties there. Everyone's more private today. The younger ones. Before, the young set all went to the Trocadero, to Ciro's, and all those places.

BH: **Now they've all closed down or been changed to new places.**

MM: Yeah, but even places like Ciro's, before that, were something else. Ciro's used to be the Club Seville.

BH: **I've never heard of that one.**

MM: It was pretty famous for the dance floor, on account of it was made of glass and it was up top of a pool full of goldfish [carp]. It finally closed down because too many ladies complained that they felt peculiar about the fish looking up their skirts! [Laughs.]

BH: **Rather peculiar women.**

MM: So Ciro's put in a regular dance floor, and everybody was happy.

BH: **Do you consider yourself a prude? If I may ask.**

MM: No. Do you?

BH: **No!**

MM: Funny thing—nobody does. But I don't hold with foul language. That's why I won't see most of the new movies. They're filthy, and not just the words.

BH: **It is true that your father opposed your becoming an actress?**

MM: It certainly is. It's why I changed my name.

BH: **Think how many would-be actresses didn't oppose their fathers....**

MM: Probably spent the rest of their lives wondering what might have been.

BH: My mother might have been one of them. She had the looks that she could have been a leading lady, but her father wouldn't have allowed it, and she says she willingly went along with his wishes. I don't think she was that keen on acting.

MM: No. If you're as keen as I was, you'd go ahead and do it. Got no choice.

BH: You did vaudeville, as well?

MM: I'm glad you heard of it! It's dead as a doornail, now. Few years ago, a lady friend said to me that her nephew asked her where vaudeville was...he thought it was a town. [Laughs.] But first I joined a stock company, and I went on working my way up, to Broadway. I played the Palace. Also did the Chautauqua circuit...I got around.

BH: Was it very challenging, being a woman traveling the country on her own in those days?

MM: First off, I'd prefer to be called a lady. In those days, a woman was somethin' else. [Winks.] Second, it weren't easy, but it wasn't like nowadays, with rape and muggings and all the crime. Men had more respect in those days.

BH: That reminds me. I have a quote from you. Could you confirm it? "Men and liquor—them's what's wrong with the world!"

MM: [Giggles.] It's a mite strong, ain't it? Liquor, of course, that's a calamity. But men're okay when they know how to behave. Gents are fine, on their side of the fence. But when they go tom-cattin' after women, and it's *women* they usually go after, then it's trouble. And everybody pays.

BH: There was much more segregation of the sexes, wasn't there?

MM: A good thing, too! I don't hold with all this barrier-breaking where the gals're entering the men-only clubs and trying to join all the men's organizations. I'm for equal financial opportunities for ladies, but if the men want to be alone, I say leave 'em alone! Most men get too preoccupied to treat a gal like a lady if they're around us all the time.

BH: By "preoccupied" you mean...?

MM: Carnal thoughts.

BH: And if men and women mix at every turn...?

MM: Then it's frustrating for the men and a burden on the ladies. And it only results in a lot of fornication. Nature's bound to take its course eventually.

BH: So you prefer men on one side and women on another?

MM: Nope. I prefer the ladies on one side and men on the other. We got our ways in common, and they got theirs.

BH: In reading about you, what surprised me was that, after the break with your father —

MM: He didn't disown me or anything like that!

BH: What I meant was that after pursuing your acting career despite such fundamental opposition, you gave up your career for another man, and one old enough to be your father.

MM: By then I was past thirty.

BH: You mean you'd passed your professional prime.

MM: Well, I was thirty-and-some.

BH: And not a leading lady.

MM: That was on account of my type. I wasn't exactly a star. But I didn't become an actress to become a star. Folks didn't think that way then. You joined the profession for the excitement, hoping you could make a living at it and see the world.

BH: See America?

MM: That was the world then.

BH: You met Dr. Krebs, a psychologist....

MM: There was lots of teams in those days—two men, a gentleman and a lady, sometimes two ladies. In vaudeville, mostly. Specialty acts. The doctor and me teamed up, and we toured the country, him giving lectures and me taking care of things. Like I say, I've been around some.

BH: Was that the golden age of psychiatry and psychology, what with Jung and Freud?

MM: [Laughs.] They did okay for themselves, but here in America, men like Dr. Krebs was thought of by most people like magicians or...experts on the occult. People wanted to know more about the subject, that's why they went to lectures. But a lot of 'em thought it was all malarkey or even paganism.

BH: So a lecture by Dr. Krebs had curiosity value?

MM: You'd have pickets outside, sometimes. Some places, mostly little towns and sometimes big ones like Boston, they tried to fix it so Dr. Krebs couldn't lecture 't all.

BH: Didn't he think of private practice or a post at a university?

MM: He could've done that, and he didn't tour all the time, but he wanted to see the world.

BH: Were you his secretary, as it were?

MM: [Slightly offended.] We worked together. He was in the spotlight, and I was behind the scenes. Taking care of things, like I said. Besides, he didn't tell me to swear off acting. And acting wasn't all I done. I taught too, you know.

BH: What did you teach?

MM: Acting. In Paris, Kentucky, at Bourbon College. [Smiles.] Bourbon....Students liked me, too. I got fired. Asked for a raise. They didn't have women's lib then.

BH: Weren't you a lecturer, as well?

MM: I was. [Beams.] Shakespeare, Dickens, the classics. I did readings....I did do some secretarial chores, correspondence and all, but I never set my sights on being a secretary or working inside an office. I was also a booking agent for Dr. Krebs — I kinda ran things.

BH: You married in what year?

MM: Let's see...1921.

BH: Was it a happy marriage?

MM: It had its ups and downs.

BH: Did the age difference matter much?

MM: It was advantageous, from where I stood. Dr. Krebs was about fifty-seven and he was mostly concerned with his lecturing. I liked lecturing — my father was a minister and all — and I thought it was a nice way to spend your time and see new places.

BH: At over thirty, did you feel it was now or never in terms of finding a man to wed?

MM: There's always old men ready to marry younger girls. Depends what you want out of life. I was ready to see what it was like to have somebody take care of me, for a change.

BH: Were you looking for a father figure?

MM: I reckon. But not a father. I wasn't searching for somebody to try and lead my life for me or tell me acting was the devil's profession.

BH: But it sounds like, as you said, you ran things....

MM: Dr. Krebs wasn't a very practical man. I didn't figure on having to run the show, I kinda tired of it after a few years. We lived in New York [City] in between tours, and I got to pining for the legitimate theater.

BH: **Reading between the lines, I gathered there was some trouble in the marriage, and that you then returned to acting?**

MM: [Agitated.] I'd like to read them lines what you read in between of! They got a nerve. That sort of thing's private. They don't know what went on.

BH: **But you did return to the, uh, arms of Thespis?**

MM: Yeah, I was an actress again. I worked with the stars before they was stars.

BH: **Mae West. Who else?**

MM: [Barbara] Stanwyck in *Burlesque* [1927]. Hits, flops, but it was steady. Most every play needs a mother type, someone who looks like me.

BH: **Meanwhile, how was the marriage doing?**

MM: He was okay. He slowed down in his sixties.

BH: **Did divorce ever enter your thoughts?**

MM: Yep. But I wasn't gonna do it. When I got married, I got married to stay. Nobody wanted a divorce, back then.

BH: **Even if a marriage turned out to be a mistake?**

MM: People looked down on divorced women. It was a disgrace, though in show business it wasn't so serious.

BH: **So you honored your marriage vows, but how real a marriage was it?**

MM: We pretty much went our own ways, but we was still, in the eyes of the law, man and wife.

BH: **How about in your own eyes?**

MM: Man and wife.

BH: **If you could go back in time, knowing what you know now, would you have married?**

MM: [Shakes head.] ...No, but once I got into it, I stayed the course. Marriage was more of a practical thing in them days. Now, everybody thinks on it like it's just romance or...worse. But it's also companionship and a practical arrangement. When I got married, I was old enough to pretty much guess what I was getting into. I had a good idea about Dr. Krebs; I didn't go into it blind. But I'm a one-man woman, and that's over with, thank goodness!

BH: **He died in his early seventies.**

MM: That's right.

BH: **How did you feel?**

MM: ...Like I lost a friend. Or a member of the family.

BH: **By then, you were becoming a fixture on the silver screen....**

MM: If you're gonna be a fixture, that's a mighty good place! [Snorts.] I may not have gotten as much attention or as big a build-up like the glamour gals, but even in the background, you're not exactly overlooked when you're up on that big screen!

BH: **As your friend Mae West once said, "It's better to be looked over than overlooked." Like yourself, she's a completely distinctive personality.**

MM: More so!

BH: **How do you mean?**

MM: If you want to talk about personality, she's an example of the triumph of personality—and I don't just mean that she's abstemious in her habits. She don't hold with liquor or smoking neither; the cigarettes in her pictures, those were corn silk! That's how she kept her wonderful complexion.

BH: **But not all women who don't smoke or drink have wonderful complexions....**

MM: I didn't say that's how she got it—that's how she *kept* it!

BH: **Ah. You were saying, about the triumph of personality—Mae West's.**

MM: All right. Mae's the voluptuous type. She's not exactly underfed. And she's nice to look at, but she's not in a league with most of the other blondes or redheads or brunettes this town has put up on a pedestal. People thought Mae was sexy, 'cause she *thought* sexy, and she talked that way. Now, I don't hold with tryin' to be sexy myself, never did. But that's her type. She believed in herself so much—"that way"—that she convinced everybody she was a sex personality and a beauty. 'Course, in those days a gal could be well-padded and still find work. Now they want the actresses anemic!

BH: **Were you ever vain?**

MM: Well, it ain't no sin, where Hollywood's concerned, but I wasn't, much. I like to dress well, like to be well-groomed. That's personal pride, not vanity, wouldn't you agree?

BH: **Indeed. You must have read the description of Marjorie Main given by Damon Runyon?**

MM: [Laughs heartily.] The one about my "voice like a file"? I heard it. Clever. Not exactly flattering, but he hit my type right on the head—nail on the head. He could've written it more embarrassing than it was.

BH: **Have you had many embarrassing moments in your life or career?**

MM: [Grins.] If I did, I wouldn't be about to discuss them. Not anything really embarrassing! It reminds me of some actor I heard about, they once asked if he remembered his most embarrassing incident, and he told the reporter that he did, then he paused, and then he asked the reporter for the next question! [Laughs.]

BH: **So, embarrassment is like dirty laundry?**

MM: [Nods.] You do it at home. Yessir. Though I'll give you one little incident that put a blush on my cheeks. I was once introduced as a real versatile gal, to an audience, and the fellow said I'd even taught acting in Paris! The dern fool forgot to say Paris, Kentucky. Naturally, somebody asked me about it, so it was up to me to disappoint 'em and say Kentucky, and soon after that, someone in the audience asked if I'd been *born* a hillbilly! Truth is, I came from Indiana. But folks often thought I was born a hillbilly. [Scowls.]

BH: **As opposed to play one very well on the screen.**

MM: [Dourly.] As opposed to becoming one, so far as too much of the public's concerned!

BH: **It's surprising how often audiences want to think an actor is her or his most frequent character, isn't it?**

MM: It's stupid! After all, it's *acting*. I got to play somebody colorful; I'm not that colorful myself.

BH: **Refined can't compete with raucous?**

MM: I mean, I'm not exactly dainty, never said I was. But they wanted a battle-ax, and I was one of the best battle-axes in the business!

BH: **That's quite a word to apply to a woman, or anyone.**

MM: I like it. It's a weapon, right? Means I can take care of myself. I never was the helpless, frilly type.

BH: **Did you mind doing mostly comedy parts?**

MM: I wouldn't want to have done all them kissing scenes! That sort of thing....I'd like to have done some Shakespeare, Molière, and the high-toned stuff. I guess it wasn't in the stars. By and large, I don't have many regrets.

BH: **You worked with W.C. Fields?**

MM: Yes. He drank....

BH: **Possibly the funniest man in movies, yet a chronic alcoholic. Did that manifest itself when you worked with him?**

MM: I didn't get that close to him. Though he had quite a roving eye, and he even tried to flirt with me!

BH: You've worked with a lot of them. May I name a name, and then you give me a thumbnail impression or reaction?

MM: Shoot! [Laughs.] I got nothin' to lose now. I ain't gonna work with any of 'em again!

BH: Fred MacMurray.

MM: [Pained expression.] I played a hillbilly in that [*Murder, He Says*, 1945]! Lotsa people seen it, over the years....

BH: And Fred MacMurray?

MM: [Giggles.] Sorry. Plum forgot. We worked together, some. He's okay...not much warmth there, as best I can remember. It's so long ago.

BH: Lou Costello.

MM: I know he couldn't stand Abbott, and he tried to change the team's name to Costello and Abbott, but the studio wouldn't have it. He was okay. Not nearly so funny in person.

BH: Lots of funny people are said to be less than humorous in person.

MM: Yeah, and you're talkin' to one! [Laughs.] But I don't take myself too serious, never did.

BH: Unlike who, for instance?

MM: The women's more touchy about it than the men. I hear Lucy's pretty stone-faced in person and also on the set, off camera-range.

BH: Didn't you work with Lucille Ball?

MM: ...You're right! I did! And I'm right—she's not so funny in person.

BH: Who else?

MM: Joan Davis. I knew her, not too well, but...she was real popular, and then she switched over to TV [in "I

Married Joan"], but she weren't none too easy to get along with — with other gals, that is.

BH: Do you think many comediennes are touchy because they're considered less feminine than more conventional leading ladies and supporting actresses?

MM: I think that's it. You hit the nail on the head. A gal what ain't a beauty is sensitive about that, if her face is famous. When you're supposed to be funny or some kind of clown, or even make fun of yourself...it ain't easy.

BH: The few stand-up female comics, like Phyllis Diller and Joan Rivers, are very self-deprecating.

MM: Yeah. They're funny. But I wouldn't do that, even if I could. They can have it!

BH: Another unliberated pattern among many female comics is the man-hungry "old maid."

MM: Yeah, the crazy spinster. The pants-chaser. Like that gal [Rose-Marie] on "The Dick Van Dyke Show."

BH: Or Joan Davis, or Eve Arden. The irony is that, often, the real women behind the comic facades are lesbians.

MM: Well, Spring [Byington] never did any of that. Her type was light comedy, and she was much more dignified. I s'ppose it depends on what a gal's willing to put up with.

BH: Or how closeted she's willing to be. Forever chasing a man on the big or little screen is a very effective cover, as far as the public's concerned.

MM: You're right, it is.

BH: What about Eve Arden?

MM: She never got her man, either! [In films, or in "Our Miss Brooks."]

BH: What about her real-life story? All about Eve?

MM: She's alive. I'm not gonna talk about her.

BH: The marvelous Edna May Oliver is long since deceased. Did you ever hear rumors about her?

MM: They wasn't rumors. It was true. And since she passed on before the war [WWII] ended, I can say it with a clear conscience. She preferred the ladies. She had a good lady friend. [Smiles.] Though she did have one husband, and I don't know what sort he was....

BH: I'm sure when a woman who's lesbian has or has had a husband, people wonder what kind of man he was....

MM: ...Well, let's not talk about that.

BH: Anyway, my friend Monica will be very happy to hear about the late, great Edna May Oliver.

MM: She was a wonderful actress. Very funny. But lots of dignity. Who's Monica?

BH: A lesbian friend at the university. A student.

MM: Oh. That's nice. She says so?

BH: Absolutely. We were talking archaeology, and I said I'd had my thirteenth birthday in Athens, and Monica said she always wanted to visit the Greek Islands, especially Lesbos, and my eyebrows must have jumped, and then she said, "I'm a lesbian."

MM: [Riveted.] Really? Just like that....Would you know she was, if she hadn't've told you?

BH: I don't think so.

MM: It's queer, in a way. [Smiles.]

BH: What is?

MM: There must be Lesbian men—on that island! [Both laugh.]

BH: Would you say a lot of the comediennes in movies have been lesbian?

MM: Yep, and are. And also on the TV—a lot of the gals playin' nurses or secretaries or maiden aunts.

BH: Like...Miss Hathaway on "The Beverly Hillbillies"?

MM: [Nods.] So I've heard.

BH: Or the —

MM: What were you askin' me, before?

BH: Back to your costars. Fred Astaire.

MM: Great dancer.

BH: Of course. But as a person?

MM: He knows he's a star....Next one.

BH: Humphrey Bogart.

MM: He was all right. You asking me about him or the movie we did? That's the one that got me goin', you know — *Dead End*. I played his mother. Called him "ya dirty yellow dog."

BH: And slapped him!

MM: Not many people slapped him, he always played a gangster. He wasn't a big star back then [1937]. The movie did a lot for us.

BH: Gloria Swanson. That film's title was *Music in the Air*?

MM: That was my first big movie part. I started in '32, but I did *Music in the Air* the next year, and it was one where I'd already done the play. That doesn't happen much anymore. But I was in the play *Dead End* — it went over a year — on Broadway. And the last stage piece I done [in 1936] was *The Women*, and they put me in the movie [1939]. Cukor directed.

BH: And Gloria Swanson?

MM: She'd have directed if she could! [Giggles.] Busy little bee. Buzzing here, buzzing there, full of suggestions. I'm surprised the director, whoever he was, could finish the picture without our star in the driver's seat!

BH: Barbara Stanwyck.

MM: That was *Stella Dallas* (1937), and I played the mother, and it's one of the biggest hits I was ever in.

BH: I notice you didn't say—and many would—"...one of my biggest hits."

MM: [Smiles.] I'd be pretty unrealistic if I did! I was too old to try and fool myself that way.

BH: **Stanwyck.**

MM: Well, I'd known her already, worked with her, and I wasn't a threat to her. So she took to me. She was nice.

BH: **Not a threat? Because of the age difference?**

MM: Yeah. We wasn't up for the same roles or types, and she felt comfortable around me. Didn't have to keep her guard up.

BH: **Do you think some major actresses, like Stanwyck or Davis, became very tough through constantly having to keep their guard up?**

MM: Yeah, it just becomes second-nature to 'em.

BH: **Clark Gable.**

MM: I liked him. He pretended to flirt with me. [Smiles.]

BH: **What about those men who actually flirted with you? Did you like that?**

MM: Who was 'e? [Comically.] Whatisname? Look, there wasn't—I mean there weren't—many of those. And no, I didn't like it. With Gable, he was a big star, so it was pretend, and like a compliment. But real flirtin's like taking something for granted, and men can be pretty crude. Politeness is fine. Flirtin'—that's somethin' else again!

BH: **Ronald Reagan.**

MM: The governor? Won't talk about him. Politics and religion...'specially politics. It gets people riled.

BH: **Spencer Tracy.**

MM: I hate to say it, but the biggest drunk in Hollywood. [Shakes her head.]

BH: **A big talent?**

MM: Yeah. He played the kind of feller you'd never know was a drunk. But he was always the same, from picture to picture, and he got offered a lot wider range of parts than somebody what wasn't a star.

BH: **I don't recall him ever using an accent in his acting.**

MM: Me neither. He was a star, and that's what the public wanted from him—they just wanted Spencer Tracy.

BH: **Actresses get much more emotional range in their roles, don't they?**

MM: Yeah—leading ones.

BH: **How many movies did you do?**

MM: Somebody once said seventy or eighty. That's a lot. [Impressed.]

BH: **Was it widely known in Hollywood in the 1930s and forties that actresses like Garbo or Jean Arthur, to name two, were lesbian?**

MM: People talked. People knew. They didn't talk about it much. Not around me. I wonder why now....Maybe if I'd gone out and around more than I did....After Dr. Krebs died, I enjoyed being on my own again, and I took advantage of it. Stayed in my own house, did as I dern well pleased!

BH: **Other than Spring Byington, were you friends with other women-loving comediennes?**

MM: I don't know that I'd call Spring a comedienne, exactly....Do you want names, or what? [Glares.]

BH: **Not necessarily.**

MM: Good!

BH: **It just seems to me that when we think of lesbian or bisexual actresses, we often think of certain stars, or European ones, such as Dietrich.**

MM: She liked men too! [Laughs.]

BH: **Bisexuality may be the norm in Hollywood.**

MM: It may be. But all that sexuality, it weren't for me.

BH: **Were you celibate?**

MM: First off, that ain't a question you ask a lady. A man, maybe. Second, it's only celibate if you have to deny yourself; not everybody's all hopped up about goin' to bed with other people.

BH: **Some people, or actresses, have low sex drives?**

MM: I reckon. Guess that's hard for a young man to believe! [Giggles.] If you was older, some of these questions might be insulting, ya know. But you wanted to know about my lady friends, and most of 'em wasn't actresses. Anyhow, most of the sapphics I heard about in Hollywood weren't homely types, they were the glamour gals.

BH: **The ones marketed as heterosexual sex symbols.**

MM: That's right. [Firmly.]

BH: **Did you have any crushes on particular glamour girls?**

MM: You want to know everything, don't ya? [Laughs briefly.] I liked Kay Francis. She was a real glamour gal, and an American, and she wore the most beautiful clothes. Had a lot of style. I always heard she was queer for the ladies. I also liked Hedy Lamarr. So beautiful! Not much talent, and she liked men. She was from Europe, somewhere.

BH: **Neither had a very long career. What about a long-running legend like Dietrich?**

MM: [Shakes head.] I liked her singing. It was sexy-like. But her whole thing, it's so artificial. The eyebrows, the whole get-up. It's phony, and she looked like a trollop half the time.

BH: **What about Garbo?**

MM: You're gonna think I'm prejudiced [against Continentals], but I'm not. Garbo was beautiful, and she didn't dress quite so outlandish. But she was always emotin'. All that suffering and heaving, and she weren't none too feminine when she walked about! I hear her feet's not as big as they say, but she's one gal what it wasn't hard to guess her secret.

BH: **She was androgynous, wasn't she?**

MM: She was what?

BH: **Both genders. Neither gender.**

MM: Well, I think every gal that preferred women fell in love with Garbo, except me! I did like her voice, though. Never did much care for high-pitched dames.

BH: **Like?**

MM: Like Kathryn Grayson, and that's all you're getting out of me! [Laughs.]

BH: **What do you think of lesbian-themed films like *Maedchen in Uniform* or *The Killing of Sister George*?**

MM: I don't know those two. What's that first one?

BH: **It was a pre-Nazi German film, directed by a woman, set in a girls' school.**

MM: I seen *The Children's Hour*. That had a school. Didn't like the ending.

BH: **In which Shirley MacLaine, as Martha, hangs herself after confessing she's in love with Audrey Hepburn.**

MM: I don't think it's a proper ending. The lesbian could've just moved someplace else.

BH: **It's a very propagandistic ending. Did you see Barbara Stanwyck in *Walk on the Wild Side*?**

MM: Sure did! She was great in it.

BH: **And brave to do it. Though they did give her a husband, for a safety net.**

MM: She's so different now than when I worked with her.

BH: **Harder?**

MM: ...A lot more butch.

BH: **She made quite a matriarch in [the TV series] "The Big Valley."**

MM: I liked that one!

BH: **You'd have been wonderful in something like "Green Acres" or "Petticoat Junction."**

MM: [Grimaces.] Think so? I'm glad you didn't say "The Beverly Hillbillies." I liked that one, too, but I wanted to stay retired, and I didn't want to keep repeatin' myself.

BH: **Couldn't you have done guest shots on those shows? It would have been a real treat for your fans.**

MM: That's sweet of ya. But when I quit, I quit cold turkey.

BH: **Why?**

MM: Why? Well,...for one thing, Ma and Pa Kettle helped prop up Universal, made them a lot of money. My two last pictures where I didn't play Ma Kettle was *The Long, Long Trailer* with Lucy [and Desi], a real big hit, and *Friendly Persuasion*. That was with Gary Cooper. And I starred, or costarred, in all nine Kettles, so how was I goin' to top myself? Besides, I didn't want to have to scrounge around for work, not at that age. If I really did seventy or eighty movies, it was time for me to move on!

BH: **You certainly earned it.**

MM: I reckon. But not just that. Television didn't do much for the movies. Ruined them, pretty near. After television came in and took over, the movies got worse—morally, too—and it got tougher to make a living in pictures. You worked less, you didn't have a studio behind you, and if you were much older than a teenager, you weren't in style anymore!

　　I worked during the best part of Hollywood, and I still feel I got out at a good time.

BH: **Do you travel much now? Or do you feel you've seen the world?**

MM: [Laughs.] They say the world's gettin' smaller. Not to me, it ain't. It's huge! And frightening. Mostly, I travel between here and Palm Springs. Got a home there. It's a nice trip, and a nice change of scenery and climate.

BH: **Do you like westerns?**

MM: What brought that up?

BH: **The Palm Springs terrain. Ideal for cowboys. Or cowgirls.**

MM: I like to watch 'em, yeah.

BH: **What do you think of *Johnny Guitar*, if you've seen it?**

MM: The one with [Joan] Crawford? That was something else! So was her adversary, that other gal [Mercedes McCambridge]. I could see that one again. [Laughs.]

BH: **It was made in 1954. Do you think that two decades later, the lesbic undertones are more noticeable to audiences?**

MM: I noticed, first time I saw it! You can't help it, when the two gals are so derned butch!

BH: **Did their image appeal to you?**

MM: Not that other one. She's too ornery. But Crawford always looks good. Even in pants. I'm a bit too big in the caboose for pants!

BH: **Another unusual western was *The Furies*, same decade, with Barbara Stanwyck. Have you seen it?**

MM: Yes. Walter Huston played her father.

BH: **And he prefers his butch daughter to his son, but Judith Anderson comes between father and daughter. Do you remember the big scene?**

MM: The big scene? Oh! My gosh—that was horrible. I'm surprised Stanwyck agreed to do it [her character throws a pair of scissors at Anderson, Huston's fiancee]. I'm agin it. That gives ideas to people who got no business gettin' ideas into their heads. It's violent, and it's for violence.

BH: **Did you notice that Stanwyck's character never got punished for disfiguring and paralyzing Anderson?**

MM: That's plum wrong....You mean, also, on account of she's a woman?

BH: **Don't you think if Stanwyck had thrown the scissors at a man, she would have had to pay?**

MM: I don't think, I know. She would've.

BH: **A double standard, wasn't it?**

MM: Still is.

BH: **When a potentially sapphic character appeared on screen, do you think that was a big thrill for most secretly lesbian women in the audience?**

MM: Well, of course. Till the character got punished. She always did. Well, not always—sometimes she got sent away. I remember one picture, the characters. Lauren Bacall was the queer gal, Doris Day was the good girl, and Kirk Douglas was glad when Bacall went away and he settled down with Doris Day. [*Young Man with a Horn*, 1950.] I'm just talking about who they played....

BH: **Were there whispers or rumors that the great director Dorothy Arzner was lesbian?**

MM: First off, I don't think people thought about directors as great. They didn't get all this press in those days. Arzner sure didn't. That was *long* ago....If she got any attention paid her, it was on account of everyone thinking how strange it was for her to do what she was doing. But I did hear it told that she wasn't keen on men. She looked more like a man than any actress what they ever let work in front of a camera, so it wasn't a big revelation. If a gal even wanted to direct pictures, that there was a good tip-off to where her personal interests was.

BH: **You mean that a heterosexual woman wouldn't wish to direct?**

MM: Not in those days. Not most of 'em.

BH: **What has changed that?**

MM: I don't know that it has. I think Miss Arzner just couldn't hide the fact [of her lesbianism]. She didn't bother to. Didn't get herself a husband.

BH: **Do you think that killed her career, eventually?**

MM: Most likely. But all that stuff gets hushed up. No one ever admits to it. They give other reasons.

BH: **Like "creative differences"?**

MM: That's the usual one.

BH: **What do you think of lesbians who marry men?**

MM: I think they're ambitious.

BH: **Isn't it a big price to pay?**

MM: Depends on the man. They might not be together most of the time, or in any sense of the word.

BH: **You mean a, um, white [celibate] marriage?**

MM: That. And they might live in different houses or different wings of the same house. The same address don't necessarily mean much.

BH: **Haven't stars like Garbo [who never wed] proven that an actress needn't undertake matrimony for her popularity?**

MM: Yeah, but if she doesn't, she needs to get herself a man she's supposed to be in love with. They got to publicize it a lot. Like with [John] Gilbert. Gilbert and Garbo — folks thought of them as a team. Thanks to MGM.

BH: **It's simpler than marrying the guy.**

MM: [Laughs.] Not to Garbo. After that, she didn't let the studio team her with any of her co-stars. She wouldn't go out with them or be photographed with them. Gilbert was the only time she let that happen, and it was early on.

BH: **If you'd been a classical beauty, would you have considered a husband for show?**

MM: [Laughs.] If I'd been a beauty, I might be somebody different! No telling what I'd be like or what I'd consider! But if I hadn't been a mother type, or the comedic type, then the studio would have put the screws on me, and I'd have been pressured into marrying a man or at least romancing him for the publicity.

BH: A beau for show?

MM: That's how it works. And at those prices [salaries], it's hard to say no to the hand that feeds you.

BH: But now that the studio system is gone and actresses aren't under contract?

MM: They're still beholden to the public and the publicity machine. Things haven't changed *that* much. Not about *that*.

BH: But the public is far less anti-gay than it was. Why aren't we seeing any actors, on any level, relaxing their guard?

MM: 'Cause it could cost them their whole career, and who wants to go first? Nobody's got the guts to be the first. Maybe somewhere down the line, it'll be kind of accepted, but who's going to go first?

BH: Pioneers pay the highest price.

MM: Everyone's got excuses....

BH: What do you mean?

MM: When you're new, you want to keep all the doors open, so you cooperate. When you've made it, you want to be popular, you want to make it bigger still. Then when you're older, and even if you're gettin' smaller roles, you got hopes of making a comeback, and you don't want to throw away all them years of struggle.

BH: So how old does one have to be to be open about one's life and loves?

MM: Probably dead.

BH: Hollywood be thy name.

MM: Now, don't blaspheme. [Gently.] But it's not a town founded on ideals and tolerance, it's built on making money.

BH: **And offending the smallest number of bigots possible.**

MM: Well, when it comes to that, everyone's a bigot.

BH: **So far. Less and less.**

MM: It's not gonna change much in my generation. [Shakes head.]

BH: **What has a mature lesbian or bisexual actress got to hide or to be ashamed of?**

MM: Nothin' to hide, most likely. Unless she lives with her girlfriend. Even that's okay, if you got respectability. Lots of ladies live together, and it ain't always a love situation, but even when it is, nobody asks. They might wonder, but they don't pry.

BH: **But why does an entire generation seem ashamed of being different in their loves or affections?**

MM: Because they are. We've all been taught the same things. It's hard to ignore. Even if you do, no one else will. It's either your family or your employers. Or it's the public. It's hard to change how everyone feels, when it's so deep in them.

BH: **It's even deeper when everybody thinks that no one is gay or lesbian — no one they know personally.**

MM: I think the different people should be honest with their relatives, if they want to. That's practical. At work, it's not. But if they're really your loved ones....

BH: **If you had parents or siblings, would you tell them today?**

MM: I wouldn't have to tell 'em. I'd show them — I'd just show up with my lady friend, and if I'd had it to do all over, I might live with her. I've gotten so used to living on my own, but when I was younger, I'd like to have lived with her.

BH: **Who was she?**

MM: ...Someone special.

BH: **Was there one someone, or more than one?**

MM: [Smiles.] That's for me to know and you to find out! [Laughs.] But now I've gone as far as I dare. That's that, all right? I'll shake your hand, and we'll call it a day.

Despite the unexpected and warm hug, I didn't get to meet Marjorie Main again. The *Modern Screen* feature was never mentioned. I called Miss Main twice at her home, but by the second time, it seemed evident that she had little desire to re-meet. Probably she felt she'd dared too much, possibly regretting it or even feeling guilty. For my part, I didn't mind not doing a piece that wouldn't have included the woman behind the barking, maternal facade of Ma Kettle.

I wondered if she'd ever been asked any of these questions or ever before told as much to one person, to one virtual stranger? I only hoped she didn't feel bad about her frankness, and I was tempted to call again or write and note that obviously (to me) her more personal statements wouldn't see print during her lifetime.

But I didn't. Instead, I thought of her comment that "we've all been taught the same things," the same propaganda. Which reminded me, in a different but pertinent context, of an exchange in an old Mae West movie where the star announces, "For a long time, I was ashamed of the way I lived."

The male assumes, "You mean to say you reformed?"

"No! I got over bein' ashamed...."

PATSY KELLY

(1 9 1 0 – 1 9 8 1)

Comedian Patsy Kelly was a lovable tough-gal, dumpy and saucer-eyed, typically enacting a maid. Eventually in real life, too. She was born Bridget Sarah Veronica Rose Kelly in Brooklyn. Raised in Manhattan, she would hang around the local fire station, hoping to become a fire-fighter — to her mother's horror. In *Motion Picture*, a fan magazine, she noted, "I heard that Greta Garbo goes around talking about when she used to be 'a young man.' Well, someone once asked me, 'cause I was such a tomboy, if I ever wanted to be a boy, when I was a little girl?

"I says, 'No, not really. Not one with a penis.' I was just happy bein' myself!"

Patsy's mother sent her to dancing school, where she became an accomplished tap dancer. Her big break was being hired by Frank Fay [Barbara Stanwyck's first husband] as his stooge in vaudeville.

Producer Hal Roach brought Patsy to Hollywood. Her film bow was *Going Hollywood* (1933) with Marion Davies and Bing Crosby. Patsy made more than three dozen films and worked often with, and as a foil to, beautiful blondes like Jean Harlow, Carole Landis, and Thelma Todd. "It was Hollywood's golden age," Kelly enthused. "Wall-to-wall blondes!" But Harlow died young, Landis committed suicide, and Todd was murdered by her boyfriend in 1935. Thus began Patsy's reputation as a *jinx*. It, alcoholism and her then-shocking openness about her lack of sexual interest in men, combined to keep her off-screen after 1943.

She turned to the stage, where she got minor roles that progressively shrank. When TV was born, Patsy did quiz shows, a virtual admission of unemployability for a celebrity then. In the 1950s her friend and sometimes lover Tallulah Bankhead hired her as her Gal Friday and "saved my life, you should pardon the expression."

Syndicated Hollywood and Las Vegas columnist Lee Graham was a fan and admirer of Bankhead's who, like many gay men, became part of her inner circle: "I was at one of Tallulah's cocktail parties. Very late, most of the guests had gone. Everyone had overimbibed, and the bunch of us were dissecting the topic of suicide. Tallulah was all for it, that is, the comforting idea that it's always there, in case things get too bad. 'Dahlings,' she said, 'I only wish I had the courage! I think about it every month or so.' Patsy piped up, 'I can top that. I think about it every week or so, and I ain't never been afraid of it.'

"So one of us asked, 'Then what accounts for our still having the pleasure of your company?' and Patsy said that every time she felt suicidal, she couldn't help wondering, 'But why *now*? Why not wait till things get really dramatic?' And of course life is never quite that dramatic."

By the time I met him in the late 1970s via periodicals we both wrote for, Lee was living in the Hollywood Hills and very well-connected (among others, he regularly squired Virginia Mayo, who admitted she liked gay escorts). With and independently of Lee, I tried to obtain interviews with lesbian or bisexual actresses, including Alexis Smith, Lillian Gish, Eva Le Gallienne—whose love life was splashed across 1920s newspapers—Mildred Natwick, soap star Constance Ford, Sheila "Dobie Gillis" James before she came out, an Australian singer—who wound up marrying a gay actor—and assorted TV "comediennes."

I got a few of the interviews, but none of the subjects allowed me to ask their sexual and affectional orientation. Even if the question were no more specific than "Are you right-handed, left-handed, or ambidextrous?" (The songbird appreciated "your analogy of left-handedness. Just so you don't ask me what I do with my hand!" But she wouldn't go on record.)

It was Lee who suggested I interview blithely lesbian Patsy Kelly. "She's fun, and you can keep it in your files." In time, we all became friends and lunch partners, but the first two interviews occurred in 1979 at Lee's home on Marlay Drive. He sat about ten feet behind Patsy, observing silently. The eager subject got up often for refills, or to pace and gesticulate, treating the place as her own and us as her best friends in the world.

BH: I do believe it's tougher to get an actress or even a comedian—no offense there—to admit to not being heterosexual than it is to find someone in Hollywood who'll admit to having been a member of the Communist party.

PK: [Laughs.] It's true....It's funny.

BH: It's sad. But though I barely know you, you seem so joyously open and honest and unbitter, I mean about the many lean years you suffered in the business.

PK: Honey, you mean outta the business, or on the fringes. The years were lean, but not me! Let's have a drink. What're you havin'?

BH: Gin and tonic?

PK: Me, I'd take the gin and leave the tonic. Gin's a good tonic, oh yeah.

BH: Never mix, never worry?

PK: Zat a movie line?

BH: Sandy Dennis says something similar—or exactly the same—in *Who's Afraid of Virginia Woolf?*

PK: Is she...uh?

BH: Of the sisterhood? So I've heard.

PK: I loved her in that dyke movie [*The Fox*]. She was the only thing in it that didn't reek. 'Course, she always gives the same performance.

BH: But it's a lulu.

PK: And I should talk!

BH: I'm not sure why, but it's hard for a man to ask an actress if she's gay or bi—lesbian, actually.

PK: How come, honey?

BH: Well, if a man asks an actor he *knows* is gay, usually one of two things happens: the actor denies and Antarctica sets in, or the actor tries to move the interviewer—or friend— toward the bedroom.

PK: How about a simple "yes"?

BH: "Yes, I am"? Not in America. It doesn't happen. Not in words.

PK: And if you ask an actor you think is gay and he's not,...*pow*, right in the kisser! I've known a few guys, nancy types, I thought they were members, and nope—

they were just made funny. It happens. Listen, I know plenty of dames, butch dames, *you'd* think they was members—bona fide! But—nope!

BH: **It may be easier for a female journalist to inquire into an actress's private life. An actress, be she lesbian or hetero, may think a male is coming on to her if he asks.**

PK: Honey, men don't come on to me, no way! If a guy came onto me, for the last twenty years, I'd know sure as the sun comes up, he's a lesbo! [Laughs.]

BH: **I can see—a little—why a blonde, conventional actress might hide her non-orthodox sexuality. But not why some female comic actresses I've met or been told about are equally desperate to hide their lesbianism or even bisexuality, since the whole world thinks they're butch anyway.**

PK: Butch, that's one thing, honey. Beautiful, that's another thing. Straight, dyke, AC-DC, all that's got nothing to do with either. You got beautiful dykes, you got butch hetero gals. Just because most ladies are effeminate doesn't mean they all are, and ya can't judge a book, like the saying goes.

BH: **But for instance, I met—socially—this older actress. Never played a dramatic role, ever. Always plays the man-hunting spinster, and no one in Hollywood thinks she's straight.**

PK: If you're talkin' about who I think you are, the only straight thing about her is her vodka. Is it X?

BH: **Yes.**

PK: When you said old, you weren't kiddin'. She's so old, she played the Forum. The Roman Forum.

BH: **She's very pleasant, upbeat....But when I deliberately made a pro-gay comment, thinking it would make her feel comfortable—because someone within earshot had just made a disparaging comment about a famous married les-**

bian actress—X froze on me. She put her drink down and went toward the proverbial ladies' room.

PK: Honey, that was no lady. That was a closet king.

BH: I later asked someone at the party if it was known whether X were very closeted. He said, "The only person in Hollywood who doesn't know X is a lesbian is X."

PK: [Laughs uproariously.] Honey, she knows it all right— she'd just sooner die than let anyone know she knows.

BH: But my question is this: since she'll never be playing or probably wouldn't be allowed to play a lesbian character, and since everyone in tinseltown knows she's lesbian, why such a strenuous denial even when she's off-camera and supposedly socializing? What does she think she has to lose? Not jobs—everyone *knows*, and publicly she goes along with the man-hungry charade.

PK: That's it in a nutshell, sweetie. She's got nothin' to lose. Nothin' to fear but fear itself.

BH: She is her own closet. She carries it around wherever she goes.

PK: She does. You're not telling me something I didn't know. There's only one thing she could possibly lose if she was a little more honest about herself. See, if she's honest to herself, what she might lose—ta-da!—is her...self-respect.

BH: In that case, she's defining herself by the standards of her bigoted enemies.

PK: People do stupid things in Hollywood, to fit in.

BH: Not just in Hollywood. I had a classmate from India who was here on the AFS [American Field Service] program, studying. He had a tattoo of a Hindu god or saint on his chest. I thought it was stunning.

PK: His chest or the tattoo?

BH: Now that you mention it...but a beautiful tattoo, and not big or at all gaudy. Next thing I hear, he's in Arizona or New Mexico. Studying, of course. But he's become a Christian. Why? He tells me when next we meet, and with a straight face—he's heterosexual—that he converted because those same Christians used to make fun of his Hindu tattoo!

PK: Welcome to the club. [Raises her glass in a mock toast.]

BH: Tattoo and all.

PK: Most people, if they're criticized for whatever it is that's different about 'em, if it goes on long enough, and if they're soft in the head—or low on self-respect—they get to believing what they're hearing. They might even try and join the bandwagon.

BH: The same bandwagon that's been trying to trample them.

PK: Some people can't stand criticism.

BH: Then they're not equipped for life on this planet.

PK: I'll drink to that. Me, I've heard it all, and it just don't move me. Names is a game two can play at.

BH: You must have been pressured, yet you stood your ground. You're not a closet, like Miss X, and...

PK: I never had a policy. But what I figured out for myself, way back there, was, don't say yes and don't say no. A little mystery never hurt anyone. Look what it did for Greta Garbo! Not that I had the same natural resources, mind you.

BH: Did you ever consider marrying a guy?

PK: Only for money and only when I was poor. Don't think there wasn't a few takers. I'm no prize in the Gibson Girl sweepstakes, but there's messes of guys out there, ready to tie the knot with any girl who's famous, just so's he can get in on some of that high life and publicity.

BH: **You mean because being rich is just—**

PK: Listen, I'd settle for just bein' rich! Money's okay by me! I never wanted to be the big cheese in the pickle factory. But let's face it, actors is more interesting than people like millionaires. Millionaires like to get to meet us, have us entertain 'em. Like old Hearst, when he'd invite all the biggest stars—the biggest stars, mind you, not the funny girls who played maids. He'd invite 'em up to whatsitcalled.

BH: **Xanadu. I mean *San Simeon*.**

PK: And sometimes them rich folks marry into acting. It never lasts, but it's good for a few laughs. What the hay. And for publicity. Obviously.

BH: **If you'd gotten contractually married, would you have preferred a gay husband?**

PK: Yeah....Cole Porter. But he was taken.

BH: **You wouldn't have taken on a heterosexual?**

PK: Yeah, I wouldn't. I mean no. Yeah, wait a minute: I'm a dyke. So what? Big deal!

BH: **You may be the only woman in Hollywood to say that. Congratulations.**

PK: Let's have a toast [We toast.] To honesty. It's not the best policy, but it's the *only* way to fly! Bottoms up!

BH: **...Speaking of flying, why do you think Peter Pan is always played by an actress?**

PK: I dunno why they'd try and cast it that way. But it figures why certain actresses—the sisterhood?—want to be Peter Pan. Gals like Mary Martin and Jean Arthur. They want to be boys.

BH: **You mean because Martin and Arthur are lesbians.**

PK: In a nutshell. You read *Peter Pan?*

BH: **The play or the story?**

PK: Either. Both.

BH: Both.

PK: Okay, I never read 'em. So *you* figure it out. Why do the big honchos like to cast actresses to play that Peter Pansy guy? Not that *I'm* looking to play 'im. I'm too butch to play Peter Pan—but I definitely believe in fairies! [Raises her glass.]

BH: **Clap, if you believe....From what I've read and what I deduce, Peter Pan resists the flirtations of the girls in the story—Wendy, Tinkerbell, and Tiger Lily the Indian maiden. Maybe producers or casting directors, not to mention audiences—hetero audiences, anyway—feel more comfortable, even reassured, watching an actress rebuff the advances of another actress. If Peter's an actor, then they're watching that male actor rebuff Wendy, then Tinkerbell, then Tiger Lily, and they wonder *why*....**

PK: And why Peter Pan doesn't want to grow up, why he wants to be a boy forever.

BH: **Many amateur psychologists—and that includes the professional ones—would say his refusal to grow up is a refusal to be heterosexual. I think not. Alexander the Great and Leonardo Da Vinci were hardly arrested cases.**

PK: If they came back, they might be....

BH: **Beg pardon?**

PK: Arrested. One too many wild parties...?

BH: **Clever. Everyone's heard that a huge percentage of comedians are Jewish. What no one ever says is how big a percentage of female comedians are lesbian. Why is that?**

PK: A lot are. The stand-ups. It takes that macho kind of defiance of an audience, of hecklers and what people think of you, to be a lady stand-up. But let me tell you: the few comediennes that's made it big—you can count 'em on one hand—they're not the dykes. Diller and Rivers ain't dykes. And Bea Lillie, that's a different ket-

tle of fish, 'cause she's English, so she can get away with
moiduh [murder], and she got married and had a kid, so
she's some honorary heterosexual lady or something.

BH: And she literally is a lady. Lady Peel, because she married
a baronet. I *think* he was a baronet.

PK: I thought he was a coronet.

BH: So the question is, why are so many women comedians
gay?

PK: I know this—the best lady comics are mostly dykes. I
don't much go for that puttin'-yourself-down routine,
like Diller and Rivers is always doin'. It's okay in real
life, a little, to break the ice, but it gets stale fast on a
stage.

BH: Do you think when a would-be actress like X is plain or
not particularly feminine...

PK: I never knew an effeminate comedienne yet, honey.

BH: ...that she instead goes into comedy by default?

PK: It's logical. If you look like Lana Turner, you don't need
a sense of humor. Life is kind. So are men and kids.

BH: Until you refuse them.

PK: Right! Men don't like no for an answer. *No*'s supposed
to be the masculine word, and *yes* means feminine or
whatever. What the hay.

BH: Who's your favorite actress, besides Tallulah?

PK: Honey, Tallu ain't my favorite actress. Listen, I'm loyal
to her, but I got my own opinions. But lemme keep this
to myself. I got all these fabulous ladies I love. I'm the
biggest fan in movies. I'm probably the first and oldest
movie buff! I'd rather talk about this special field of
interest. I never get asked about it. Anyone can do
movie chatter.

BH: What woman do you admire a lot, and why?

PK: Delilah. No, I'm spoofin'. Just kiddin'. Real-life woman, huh?...Margaret Mead, she's a doctor, isn't she?

BH: Yes.

PK: Then her. Any lady doctor's aces with me. But ya know, "Doctor" fits in front of "Margaret." It doesn't sound right in front of "Patsy"!

BH: You worked with and were a friend to Jean Harlow. Do you think she was an exhibitionist?

PK: Yeah, in an innocent way. She learned fast she could turn men on, or up. So she'd ice-cube her nipples, she wouldn't put on underwear....But it was strictly look-don't-touch. For a platinum bombshell, she didn't have many affairs. She preferred to do it inside of marriage. But she was scared to have a baby; she said so to me.

BH: Hard to believe that in early Hollywood, actresses were discouraged from having babies, sometimes discouraged from marrying and disappointing their admirers.

PK: Now, every marriage, baby, divorce, and remarriage is good for a year's worth of publicity. Brother!

BH: Did you have a crush on Jean?

PK: The Pope Catholic? But what could I do about it, besides what millions of her other fans did at night, alone....Everyone called her "the baby," and the baby didn't know from lesbians, honey. In those days, that was still possible.

BH: Which must have made it lonely and frightening for young women realizing their affectional and sexual orientation?

PK: It was frightening, I'm sure it had to be. But not for me, really. I knew how I was, I knew that was that, and I didn't think it was so bad. Not next to what my mother had to go through. I knew *I* wasn't getting stuck with some boozer—sure, him enjoyin' the liquor and then takin' it out on me! That'd be the day! I wanted to run away and join a circus, be on my own. My big aim was to be a fireman—they didn't call 'em firepersons, honey, not then!

I'd spend my spare time around the fire station, and the chief noticed me, asked me why I was there so often, and when he saw I was a girl, and I said I wanted to join the team, he sent me to my mother, and she stuck me in a dancing school, but I said if it was that ballet crap, I wasn't goin'. It wasn't, and I became a tap dancer, and that's the start of this little professional saga. But I'd rather refill my drink. How's your drink?

BH: **Still here. Thanks. Did your mother take it hard that you didn't marry?**

PK: I think she'd've been sorry for the poor shmuck! 'Cause probably I'd be the one enjoyin' the booze and takin' it out on *him*, after! I knew it would be a mean thing to do to a guy; I also knew the first time he'd raise his hand to me would be the last time. It was...everywhere. You heard the neighbors, the wives and kids crying and screaming. Now they call it wife-beating, then they called it marriage. And the husbands got away with it.... Oh yeah, it was bad.

BH: **Did you have any siblings?**

PK: Well, I don't know, but I had a brother. He was raring to get into show business, and I went along on an audition with him. Anything to get out of the house! I went along, and *I* got the job, not he! Listen, it happens. Could I help it? I was born funny, in more ways than one, and it was destiny—if I couldn't be a cop or put out fires, I'd be up there makin' people laugh. I made people laugh, bein' a mouthy little thing. I wasn't anything like Shirley Temple or those other little sugarpots you saw in the movies, so at least I wound up getting paid good money for makin' people laugh.

BH: **And you didn't have to do it by saying you were, say, flat chested or unpopular with boys.**

PK: Nope. I was a domestic, an uppity, loud, butch maid. A scaredy-cat. Remember that movie, *The Gorilla* [1939]? That was what I did. If they had to show one representative clip, they could show me in *The Gorilla*. I was there to liven up the proceedings and give 'em a little low humor. That's why my roles were pocket-sized; a lot of me would have been like a tidal wave; the males wouldn't have known what hit 'em.

That's why when I did bigger roles, they had to pair me with another actress. Somebody more...all that Hollywood stuff: pretty and feminine, a lady who couldn't open her mouth too wide. I always had a big mouth, and it says purtnear whatever my brain is transmitting. No wonder I got fired so much. I had to learn to keep still — "like a lady," to use a phrase my mother knew by heart. So I'd be quiet and lady-like, and still they'd fire me, or they wouldn't hire me, and I decided, fuck it — as long as these guys are gonna push me around anyway, I'll damn well say what's on my mind. 'Cause it feels good!

Before the initial interview, Lee Graham had advised me, "Patsy jumped at this chance to be interviewed. She doesn't do many. It's because she's old news already. Editors want young or big stars. Also, being a lonely person, Patsy tends to make a fool of herself during some interviews. Particularly if the interviewer is a cute young lady."

Afterwards I asked Lee if he felt she'd behaved and spoken in character during our interview. "With you, she was a perfect gentleman," he said. After our second interview, I offered Patsy the chance to listen to the recordings. "Honey, this voice of mine ain't exactly my favorite listenin' material. Just go for it, and don't erase a thing! Only, don't let me sound boring. If I'm boring, they won't hire me."

The knockabout actress, whose two latest major assignments—her last films, as it turned out—were both Disney pictures, allowed, "If I ain't raucous, they ain't interested. They hire me to be an Irish loud-mouth!" She also reiterated her concern that her candid comments not be published "till the dwarves—the Disney folks—are done with me. Hopefully never. They got gold coming out of their mouse ears!"

She had reason to be cautious. Between 1943 and 1960 Patsy Kelly made no movies. "They wouldn't have me." With almost no attendant publicity, she went into retirement and coped with "personal problems" that were never fully detailed. A lesbian near-scandal was reputed to be one cause of Kelly's banishment from the movie capital. Graham explained, "There was the jinx thing—a series of unlucky coincidences. Patsy was anything but a murderess. Her work and persona were deadpan, not deadly.

"What Hollywood really wouldn't forgive was that she went around with mannish women, wore slacks in public, cursed and swore, and told off-color jokes at lesbic bars and clubs. They figured she was a scandal just waiting to happen, so they used the excuse she's a lush, she's a jinx, and her type's passé. The word went out not to hire her.

"Remember, during the studio era, studios had the power to keep most things hushed up. If an actor was caught in bed with another man in a hotel or at the Y, it was usually kept under wraps. Unless the studio had already sucked all the financial juices out of the actor, like what happened in the 1930s with William Haines—MGM dropped him, and through Mayer's influence, Haines was kept from working at any other studio.

"It was usually more sordid for an actress, very two-sided. Robert Mitchum and Lila Leeds were arrested for pot in the late forties. It destroyed her career but helped make him more popular. Same as Errol Flynn, who after his rape trial was more popular than before. And poor Patsy, she had to go back east and live off show-biz friends who had savings. Until she landed a position with Tallulah Bankhead as her paid companion. Then Bankhead put her in her own vehicles, what was left of them. It was a smart move, because Patsy was born to play a wise-cracking maid. It's what she really became, for Tallulah.

"Then nostalgia came around, and Patsy was *persona grata* again. By then she was fat, cynical, and hooked on booze, but better late than never. She's a real trouper, a great survivor. But don't let her tough exterior fool you. Inside is a little girl who's still shell-shocked that show business can be so glamorous or so cruel."

When I first mentioned Tallulah Bankhead, Patsy's semisneer softened into a wistful little smile and her eyes sparkled, then glistened sadly. She was the first to volunteer that she was a star-struck satellite to the "Alabama Foghorn's" scorching sun. When the alleged jinx hadn't yet worn off, Patsy moved in with her in the early fifties and went to Las Vegas with her to work on Tallulah's debut there. "Guest resident" was one of the delicate terms the media used to describe Patsy's cohabitation with the unattached (to a male, anyway) star. Patsy then toured in Tallulah's stage vehicle *Dear Charles*.

"Having her for a friend was like waltzing with an atomic bomb. She was tremendous—the energy! She threw away better lines than Neil Simon ever wrote. She could swear so as to shake the building, and would be a great and gracious hostess. Her idea of poverty was having to run her own tub. In all kinds of weak plays, the magic of her name brought crowds to the theater. I was with her in *Dear Charles*. No masterpiece!"

Patsy did occasional theater on her own, but preferred Tallulah's company—they were tight friends through the 1950s. In 1960 Kelly made her screen comeback as—what else?—a maid in the Doris Day vehicle *Please Don't Eat the Daisies*. Her biggest film hit was *Rosemary's Baby* (1968), as Laura Louise, a witch. "Maids and witches—typecasting!" she shrieked amiably.

Her real comeback, in 1970, was the saucy maid Pauline in *No, No, Nanette*, starring her childhood pal Ruby Keeler. For Broadway, Patsy had "dieted away my flab" and become what columnist Earl Wilson called "a maid for all reasons." The musical's two-year run was followed by another hit in Debbie Reynolds's *Irene* and its tour. Thereafter, Patsy worked on TV, portraying a mother—"They should hand me an Oscar or its equivalent!" she quipped—and in Disney movies.

But Patsy credited Bankhead with sustaining her during the years when "I could do nothing right" by show people. "Tallu even called me her lucky charm, and she didn't give a good goddamn what anyone thought about our affiliation!" Patsy confessed that "I could have had more ambition and more drive. But there was even more typecasting in them days.

"What did I know? I was butch before they had a name for it. I thought they liked me anyway. I thought I could go on playing maids forever. It was the nuts! Gravy....I got paid just as much for the crummy movies as the good ones. And I didn't save a dame—I mean a dime! I was just happy, living. How did I know my career was gonna go into a coma?"

Patsy died of cancer at the Motion Picture Country Hospital near Los Angeles, a very young seventy-one. A few weeks before, she recalled with a grin, "People used to ask me about all the parties and orgies that went on in Hollywood; I'd say, 'I don't know—they never invited me.' I had to make my own fun. Now, if I can't love, at least I can laugh, and I really mean to try, until the bitter end."

BH: **I'm fascinated—tell me about Tallulah.**

PK: Honey, that's like sayin' "Tell me about Asia!" It's one big subject! Whaddya wanna know?

BH: **I've read all the books. So, things not in the books....**

PK: You musta read that on her luggage she used TBB for her monogram. It was legit. In those days, TB—the disease [tuberculosis]—was scary and a bad word. So she couldn't very well use TB for her initials. Although most people said TB really stood for Total Bitch.

BH: **Was she very bitchy? She seems to have had a good heart.**

PK: A great, big, genuine heart. She was generous, but God, if she didn't need to be the eye of the storm! Tallu was at her best in a crisis, and she manufactured 'em.

BH: **Her way of commanding attention?**

PK: Yeah, that, but she had this...she did have a self-destructive streak.

BH: **The talented actress who became a self-caricature?**

PK: She made light of not succeeding in this burg [Hollywood]. It took her a while to figure out that movies might not be capital-A art, but it was numero uno fame and fortune. Tallu wanted to be Dietrich or Garbo. Then she wanted to be [Bette] Davis. When Davis kept getting all Tallu's best parts in the movie translations, it went right to Tallulah's heart. 'Cause everyone may have raved about Tallu on Broadway, at the time, but years later, no one remembered her, and they only remembered Davis in the roles Tallu made great and made famous.

BH: **The stage does not confer immortality.**

PK: It don't even confer a fucking fortune! Tallu had to watch her pennies there at the end. She'd been such a soft touch, and she always lived high on the hog.

BH: **For her day, she was very honest about her bisexuality. That famous line of hers, "Daddy always warned me about men and alcohol, but he never said a thing about women and cocaine!"**

PK: [Hoists her glass fondly.] Yeah...Tallu was a straight shooter. Pardon the expression. Tallulah never beat about the bush — she'd gossip about you in *front* of your back! Never behind it. You always knew where you stood with her, how she felt. All in all, damn remarkable for an actress!

BH: **Do you know the *minuet* line attributed to Tallulah?**

PK: [Cackles briefly.] Hah! It's a classic! Pity I wasn't there at that moment; I coulda dined out on that story for years. Tallu was reminiscing with some old broad, and the conversation got around to music, and the gal asks Tallu, "Do you remember the minuet?" and Tallu says, "Dahling, I can't even remember the men I fucked." [Both laugh.]

BH: **I think more great lines are attributed to her than anyone. Except maybe Mae West.**

PK: Oh, come off it! Mae West stole from everybody. The dame's illiterate, and she's got whole generations believin' she wrote her own movies. Bullshit. They just didn't have any writers' unions back then, that's all.... Another morsel about Mae: she's hetero all right, but you can't tell me a nymphomaniac like her's never had one sisterly roll in that famous bed of hers, with that famous mirror overhead. But Mae wouldn't admit to one lesbian escapade out of ten-thousand-and-one heterosexual Arabian nights. A phony is what she is—all manufactured. Tallu was the opposite—100 percent real. And what you saw was what you got; no adding and no padding! No one ever heard tall tales about Tallu being a man in drag, like they did about Mae West.

BH: **See if you agree with this. If Mae did have, say, one same-sex fling, don't you think the reason she'd deny it is that our media—not to mention the medians of median-America—are so ignorant? If a heterosexual has one gay fling, just one out of curiosity, she or he is likely to be labeled as a bisexual or, if she or he is disliked, as gay or "queer."**

PK: Yeah. That's it in a nutshell. You gotta be 100 percent one way or the other, else the opposite side starts beefin.'

BH: **Did Tallulah go to bed with Garbo?**

PK: You wanna hear somethin' funny? In those days, people didn't talk about sex so much. Engaged in it, but didn't talk after, not like today. I know Tallu had more girlfriends than Errol Flynn, but...

BH: **But women weren't as free in their sexual talk together then?**

PK: ...Here's what I'm tryin' to get across: I always say live and let live, but for a while there, Tallu and me was close, and if she'd been willin' to tell me about the big names in her not-so-secret past, possibly I wasn't so willin' to listen. There was actually a time when I had a small jealous streak. Small but sensitive.

BH: **Did you love her?**

PK: Of course I did.

BH: **It was more than platonic, wasn't it?**

PK: ...It was *beyond* platonic. In the final analysis, it's friend-ships that outlast the sexual, nonrational things. Tallu was my best friend.

BH: **I don't want to provoke any jealousy, but a number of pub-lications have said that Tallulah's best friend was Estelle Winwood....**

PK: [Takes a long swig.] Could be. That ain't contradictory of what I said. I said Tallu was my best friend. I didn't say I was her best friend. Ya dig?

BH: **Yes. She must have had a lot of friends, being the star she was.**

PK: Bein' as needy of people as she was. Look, I'm a people person, too. But with Tallu, it bordered on hysteria. She hated to fall asleep alone. Me, I might get hysterical only if I *don't* fall asleep alone—if I found somebody by my bed or especially *in* it!

BH: **Did your physical relationship with Tallulah last very long?**

PK: Honey, I'm not sayin' we went to bed for two years then swore off each other. It was off and on, and mostly it depended on Tallu's moods...and if she wasn't seein' someone else. When she'd get caught up with some man, she'd go quite hetero on us. She liked the man to think he was the latest, the lucky latest, in a long, ever-lovin' line...of just *men!* With her lady amours, she was up to talkin' about the men and the women in her boudoir derby.

BH: **Some of her famous lines indicate that, Southern lady though she was, Tallulah tried every sexual act and position.**

PK: Anything once, that was her motto. Anything more than once, if it felt good. Don't press me too much on this intimate kind of thing now, 'cause sex and booze don't mix. But Tallu sure loved pubic massages.... *What* do you think of *that*? [Done in a Bette Davis clipped voice.]

BH: **You mean, that Latin word....**

PK: Yeah. Fingers, lips, appliances, you name it. Tallu didn't just enjoy stimulatin' conversations....[Winks.] And what the hay, let's face it, I was practically her maid, and whatever milady desired, I was glad to provide. In quantity! Now, pour me a drink here, and let's sail on to the next stormy topic.

BH: **No more Tallulah?**

PK: Honey, we can talk Tallulah till the cows come home! I don't mind at all. Just lay low on the questions about in bed. I know this won't get out for years, like ya promise, but it's a little too raw. Not for me, for the Disney people.

BH: **You were in two Disney movies that I liked, I mean, as Disney movies go. *Freaky Friday* [1976] and *North Avenue Irregulars* [1978].**

PK: Ya know what they called it [*North Avenue Irregulars*] in England? [Snorts.] *Hill's Angels*. Couldn't ya die?

BH: **I could bust. I liked the idea of *Freaky Friday*, where Jodie Foster and her mom [Barbara Harris] exchange bodies.**

PK: Ain't she a boyish little actress?

BH: **I have a friend, who, when he first saw her in one of her childhood movies, swore she was a boy.**

PK: Honey, maybe she *was*. Anything's possible, nowadays.

BH: **Most tomboys don't seem to grow up to be lesbians, do they?**

PK: They don't *seem* to, is all I can say.

BH: **Back to Tallulah. She married a man, one man. How did it work out?**

PK: It didn't! Leave it to Tallu to choose a loser, when all sortsa beaux were after her. She coulda chosen a really rich one, a handsome one, one who didn't drink and had the brains to know he'd be Mr. Bankhead after they tied the knot. But...nope. [Shakes her head.] She chose a bum with good manners. I told her, afterward, "Honey, everyone's got good manners on the first date. Even the second or third date. Don't judge nobody on best behavior!" A marriage license is usually a license to take someone for granted and start pining over what's un-licensed. He cheated on her, ya know, and it wasn't even a long marriage.

BH: Who was the biggest love of Tallulah's life?

PK: Her career. No competition there, it was her career. Good thing, too, because it was the one that stayed with her and gave her some comfort, gave her dough, let her have some self-esteem. You tell me what man would have done that?!

BH: Who has been your biggest love, Patsy?

PK: Boze, you're lookin' at him—her. [Raises her glass.] Lady Liquor. We've gotten too palsy-walsy at times, but now I know just how to handle her. She's a tricky one—lovable but dangerous—and I learned her tricks the hard way. Poor Tallu was too impatient to learn 'em....[Sighs.] She went [died] in '68, and ya know, life's never been quite as fun since then. Nope, it hasn't.

NANCY KULP

(1 9 2 1 – 1 9 9 1)

Virtually everyone within TV's dominion recognized her from "The Beverly Hillbillies," which premiered in 1962 and was an instant success. In almost every one of the series' 274 episodes filmed over nine years, she appeared as Miss Jane Hathaway, emphasis on the Miss. Many people don't know that she ran for Congress in 1984, and perhaps most don't know her name: Nancy Kulp. She lives on in reruns as TV's most famous "spinster" and the sixties' most efficient and erudite secretary.

Until stereotyping and aging killed her career, Kulp played the eternal spinster. Miss Hathaway was one of the pillars of her series, but the role forever locked the thespian into "the direction I'd actually been headed since my movie debut. On paper, I began very well, and several of my silver screen credits are impressive. I worked with celebrated directors and stars who were household names.

"But the bottom line is, my movie career added up to an unsatisfying although remunerative assortment of repetitive bits and pieces."

Often described as horsey, lean, bony, dignified yet gawky, etc., Nancy Kulp was a handsome rather than beautiful woman, and tomboyish in an upper-crust, collegiate way. She was born in Harrisburg, Pennsylvania. Her father ran a private school, and the bookish Nancy majored in journalism and began graduate work before leaving to join the Naval Reserve. At twenty-two she became a WAVE in 1943. In 1945 she left the service after being promoted to junior-grade lieutenant.

Kulp spent six years as a radio and television publicist. In 1951, in her thirtieth year, she embarked on a brief and little-discussed marriage to one Charles Dacus. The wedding took place on April Fools' Day. The would-be pair parted amicably; Dacus had encouraged Kulp to give vent to "my off-and-on ambition to give acting a whirl." So she moved to Hollywood and became a film publicist. Three weeks later, a producer discovered her. "I did not have to circumnavigate the casting couch to earn my breaks," she eventually explained.

Her first break was through gay A-list director George Cukor in *The Model and the Marriage Broker* (1951). It was a role larger than those which followed, but mostly silent and rather demeaning: a forlorn young old-maid desperately seeking matrimony via a marriage broker (Thelma Ritter). The title model and film heroine was the conventionally lovely and arguably dull Jeanne Crain.

In 1954 Nancy had a bit in Cukor's *A Star Is Born*—later cut without the director's approval—and the same year played a servant who envied but cheered Audrey Hepburn in *Sabrina*. If you didn't go out for popcorn, Nancy briefly showed up in movies as diverse as *Shane*, *The Three Faces of Eve*, *Strange Bedfellows* with Rock Hudson (the other fellow was Gina Lollobrigida), and *The Parent Trap* with Hayley Mills—Kulp as a butch girls' camp troop leader.

Because she was film-cast as a type rather than an individual, Kulp was eligible for the semistardom of a recurring sitcom role on television. She was taken up by "The Bob Cummings Show" (1955-59), which also featured Ann B. Davis as the tomboyish Shultzy; Davis was later recycled as spinster Alice on "The Brady Bunch." Nancy played prim Pamela Livingstone, a bird-legged bird-watcher deemed "love-starved"—presumably for a man—but belittled by playboy bachelor Bob because she was intelligent and plain. And then came Jane....

BH: Our mutual friend suggested that either I ask you up-front what you're willing to share about your personal life or wait and conclude with the Big Question.

NK: The Big Question? It sounds ominous. [Grins.]

BH: The bigots make it a Big Question.

NK: Show business makes it the Fatal Question.

BH: Not necessarily. Are you retired from acting?

NK: Unofficially. In acting, one never says never, although I just did.

BH: Should I ask that question now, and if so, do you want me to suppress the answer—I mean from seeing print—until some future date?

NK: I'd appreciate it if you'd let me phrase the question. There is more than one way....Here's how I would ask it: Do you find that opposites attract? My own reply would be that I'm the other sort—I find that birds of a feather flock together. [Pause.] *That* answers your question.

BH: It does, and I'm glad you've allowed the question to be raised.

NK: As long as you reproduce my reply word for word, and the question, you may use it. I don't fancy that you'll find much of a market for our interview, unless it were a coming-out story, and we've agreed not to do that.

BH: Yes. But hasn't any gay or lesbian publication in recent years sought an interview with you? If not about yourself, then about Miss Hathaway's sapphic undertones?

NK: There were some feelers put out by that magazine, *The Advocate*. To cut the story short, they were unprofessional and boorish, and I was advised by people who knew those boys to avoid them like the plague.

BH: Every several months one reads in the obituaries of another *Advocate* staffer...

NK: I didn't mean it like that, of course. But there is plenty of bitchery there.

BH: What about the lesbian writers of such magazines and papers?

NK: I'm not utterly informed, you know, but I hear that gay editors at *The Advocate* and elsewhere discriminate against lesbians.

BH: Yes, I've heard of various sex discrimination lawsuits that were settled out of court.

NK: It's an inescapable pattern—heterosexual men discriminate against women, and homosexual men do the same. Most, not all.

BH: You majored in journalism. My master's degree is in journalism. Don't you think you should write your memoirs?

NK: It would be a slender volume—nothing to kiss and tell about! [Chuckles.] Not what they want to hear about.

But I know about you, and reading your book *Conversations With My Elders* is what decided me to talk with you, although I fear it won't be as long an interview as some of those I read.

BH: Your time and willingness are appreciated. I don't think I've ever read a full-length interview with you.

NK: I've done them, though not over-many. But if there isn't a bit of scandal or a lot of bitchery, they sometimes don't get published. You know, speaking of the gay/lesbian press, I think the important service they provide is reporting the sort of news that usually doesn't survive the unofficial censorship of the mainstream magazines, papers, and TV news. Because when *Time* or *Life* or TV says "human interest," they mean heterosexual human interest, exclusively.

BH: That's true. But enough about media. Let's talk about...Miss Hathaway. Why do you think everyone liked her?

NK: Did they? I'm not contradicting you. I got tons of fan mail through the 1960s.

BH: Any of it from lesbians?

NK: Few described themselves as such, then. But I could often tell. There were many letters thanking me for enacting and consistently presenting a character who had a career, was cool and competent, and seemed perfectly satisfied without a husband. Some fans said they wanted to be exactly like her.

BH: Miss Hathaway was far more competent than her boss, Mr. Drysdale. That bank couldn't have functioned without her.

NK: Yes, she called him "Chief," but she often had to take charge. Mr. Drysdale tended to lose his head during each weekly crisis. The mere mention of money, or of funds being withdrawn, was enough to send him into a catatonic fit.

BH: **I heard you didn't always get along with the actor [Raymond Bailey] who played him?**

NK: Understatement. [Drily.] He was prone to being neurotic. Part of it was sensitivity over his toupee. Some people joke that in show business a younger actress sometimes has her time of month, but an older actor always has his toupee....Our stumbling block was that Mr. Bailey viewed me as his supporting actress.

BH: **I've read that during the making of "Upstairs, Downstairs," the actors playing the masters kept aloof from those playing the servants, sometimes even treating them as such. Did Bailey treat you like his secretary or employee?**

NK: Good old-fashioned sexism! [Snickers.] That was his tendency. Happily, Miss Hathaway was not downgraded over the years. [Producer] Paul Henning realized that Jane was an integral part of the series' chemistry and ratings.

BH: **It's often said Miss Hathaway was a repressed character.**

NK: Those were repressed times. Yes, Miss Hathaway was repressed. Oh, yes. I'm not saying what she was repressed about, but she had her big, dark secret. [Chuckles.]

BH: **Why not reveal her secret, now the series is over and times aren't as repressed?**

NK: Well, it's my conviction that Miss Hathaway was not a Miss, she was a Ms. A closet feminist. Even before she knew she was one.

BH: **Just a closet feminist? Any other closets?**

NK: Well, she flirted with men. But that doesn't require over-much energy or commitment. It was expected of her—by the scriptwriters and the times. Women on the job have to bill and coo now and then.

BH: **But what gender did she fall in love with?**

NK: Aha! We don't even know she ever did fall in love. Everyone gets crushes, on either sex. But we never saw Jane Hathaway at home or in younger days. A viewer can assume anything she or he wishes. Personally, I never completely filled in Jane's background for myself. I wanted her to be able to stay fresh, not to pattern her into a routine set of reactions. She was a character, she wasn't me.

I always kept a distance between my characters and myself. Partly for self-preservation. An actor doesn't want to invest that much of herself in a character. It makes her more vulnerable.

BH: **But when, say, a heterosexual actress plays a secretary, doesn't she automatically play her as a heterosexual secretary if it's unspecified?**

NK: She might. Or she might leave the character's backstory—her past and her personal life—open to interpretation. I do know that Jane was always urging her fellow females to stand up for themselves. She always encouraged the other secretaries to stand up to the boss, she encouraged Ellie May's self-confidence, and she admired Granny. And Jane was never bitchy with other women, which is rare in comedy or drama.

BH: **Some might say that's more typical of a lesbian than a heterosexual woman. Do you think so?**

NK: I think it's realistic. Regular women compete with each other for men, and sometimes there is bitchiness. If a woman is fond of her own kind, then she's less bitchy with them, and less competitive with them. She might be competitive with men, but in the 1960s of "The

Beverly Hillbillies," Miss Hathaway was kept entirely non-threatening. She was capable and independent, but male audiences were comfortable with her.

BH: **What do you think of the crush she was supposed to have on Jethro, who was such a cretin that his hunk status hardly mattered?**

NK: That was low comedy. The opposites thing—an older, plain, intellectual woman and a younger, rather stupid but handsome yokel. The impossible dream, played strictly for laughs. I doubt anyone could picture Jane and Jethro walking down the aisle together, or would want to.

BH: **The real-life Janes would be more apt to go for Ellie May.**

NK: True.

BH: **Wearing glasses was always a part of your persona.**

NK: There's an old saying—"Men seldom make passes at girls who wear glasses."

BH: **Unless they have good frames.**

NK: Very good! [Laughs.] But I almost always wore the glasses for comic effect. For the stereotype.

BH: **And then they gave you a boyfriend, supposedly more your type, in the person of Wally Cox, of all people.**

NK: [Chuckles.] Yes. Jane was a bird-watcher, and the writers imagined that she would be ecstatic about a male bird-watcher. Of course, he was presented as a better bird-watcher than Miss Hathaway, he was an authority on the subject, and the joke was that such a mild little man was the figure whom Jane would look up to and fuss over.

BH: **He'd already become famous as TV's "Mr. Peepers." But Cox was famous in Hollywood for other reasons.**

NK: You mean being gay? I'm sure he was. Everyone said so, and I saw him flirt with a few men. What everyone talked about, although not in his presence, was his friendship with Mr. Brando.

BH: **They were roommates for a time, and in the early 1970s Marlon Brando publicly admitted to bisexuality.**

NK: I know he did, in France [while filming *Last Tango in Paris*]. I also heard that Marlon and Wally were weight-lifting partners. Cox was what one might call a slight man, but he was very well-muscled. Of course, they were usually hidden by his suits when he acted.

BH: **It was also said that Cox was more of an aggressive personality in real life, and that...well, sometimes big things come in small packages.**

NK: Is that right? So...I know that Cox was a few years younger than I, but he died sometime in the early 1970s. I wonder what he died of? It's rather extraordinary how actors, male actors, tend to die young.

BH: **While the actresses often live on and on. Another actor who died prematurely, but from a different cause, was Rock Hudson. What was he like to work with?**

NK: Professional, smooth. He seemed as though he wanted to be friendly. I mean in a platonic, brotherly way. But as though he didn't know how. I fancy that he liked me.

BH: **Do you think it was a case of kindred spirits recognizing each other?**

NK: Possibly. Obviously, I'd heard plenty about him. The stars were always talked about. Whether he knew anything about me is much less likely. I do know he didn't get along with Gina Lollobrigida, but I've no anecdotes on the subject.

BH: **You played the prim young woman....**

NK: Not that young. The *spinster*. You may say it. [Smiles.]

BH: **The spinster who mistakenly thinks that Rock Hudson is after her body and then tells him off. Something about his being a sex maniac.**

NK: About his having sex on the brain.

BH: I can't remember the movie, and anyway it was a Jerry Lewis one, but whatever it was, you were in the sporting goods department trying to buy an elephant gun, and you exploded at Lewis, as the clerk serving you, in a hilarious way.

NK: Oh, yes. *Who's Minding the Store?* [1963]. Yes, I was a great white huntress. Aggressive, bespectacled, in a man-tailored jacket, a modest skirt, sensible shoes, very no-nonsense. A female intimidating to a comic male character.

BH: **Did it hurt you when you read repeated descriptions of yourself or your characters as Plain Janes or desperate spinsters?**

NK: But it wasn't either/or. It was a confusion between performer and roles. No distinction was made—that's what first hurt about Hollywood. They don't give an actor credit for creating personality.

BH: **Yet when we see an actor in one role over and over, we often assume a connection.**

NK: I give you that. It's true. Not that I was given a choice between different types. I was always the spinster type, and inside we are aware of certain personal realities, but it's always upsetting when someone else says it out loud. Now, George Cukor gave me my real start in Hollywood. He also crushed me when he said, "Don't ever expect men to fall in love with you, except in fiction."

It's not that I needed men to fall in love with me. I wouldn't have reciprocated the feeling. But one likes to think they *might* fall in love with one.

BH: **It has to be harder as an actor. A writer's work might occasionally be criticized, but with actors it's their looks and personalities that are critiqued and labeled.**

NK: Well, they gave me every label, all the variations on "spinster" and "old maid." But the most dumbfounding thing I ever was called was "Anglo-Sexless"!

BH: **"Anglo-Sexless"?**

NK: In one of those now-defunct magazines—*Coronet* or *Pageant* or whichever. In the headline, it called me "Anglo-Sexless." [Shakes head.]

BH: **Did many people think you were English?**

NK: All the time! They also made the connection because Hathaway was the name of Shakespeare's wife, although now we wonder about the nature of that marriage, don't we? [Due to questions about Shakespeare's sexual orientation.]

BH: **May I ask a few questions about your own marriage?**

NK: I'd much rather you didn't. There's little to talk about, and no use, now.

BH: **Did you realize early on that playing spinsters was kind of a dead end, career-wise?**

NK: The first thing that got through my skull was that my being past thirty was itself an immovable career hindrance. My looks *and* my age made me an old maid by Hollywood standards. I never thought of myself as not young until my fifties.

BH: **You were lucky to land one spinster role, on "The Beverly Hillbillies," that would last you most of a decade and provide a steady income and wide exposure.**

NK: The wide exposure is a very mixed blessing. But it was sheer luck, otherwise I might never have worked after the mid-1960s, and people wouldn't even know me as "Miss Hathaway" or "Miss Jane." However, being a spinster type does hamper any real acting career. The only spinster type I know that made it to stardom is Katharine Hepburn.

BH: You're right, though being a star, especially when she was young, she was usually involved in conventional film plotting. Another actress who had a fairly long career as TV spinsters was Ann B. Davis. On "The Bob Cummings Show," as a gym teacher on "The John Forsythe Show," and as Alice on "The Brady Bunch."

NK: She also played Alice's look-alike cousin—she was a drill sergeant, if memory serves.

BH: I'd forgotten that. Did you get to know Ms. Davis well?

NK: ...Not well. If I had done, I still wouldn't talk about her. I can talk about myself.

BH: I understand.

NK: Why don't you try to interview her?

BH: I did. No chance....You know, many of yesteryear's spinsters—when gay characters weren't even permitted depiction—today can be read as closet lesbians. Like Katharine Hepburn as Jo in *Little Women* or Jane Hudson in *Summertime*, and truth to tell, most of your characters.

NK: True. One could close one's eyes to it, but it is there. If a woman is forty or more and unwed, it's by choice.

BH: Have you enjoyed your career?

NK: That is a complex question....What got me down was the small size of the roles. The repetition and the tiny bit of screen time. Often, it barely seemed worth the effort. It was more like a hobby than a career—my films [sarcastically]. Cameos, really. And no real chance of artistic growth, no dramatic potential. No dramas, actually. Just comedies.

BH: But never slapstick or total farce. You had too much dignity.

NK: It's a compensation. I was not a clown or buffoon, but in popular entertainment, a spinster or old maid is always a figure of fun. The ridicule is there, subtle or not.

BH: **Would you have played an out-and-out lesbian role, and were you ever offered one?**

NK: Yes or no depends on the quality of the script and integrity of the role. However, you forget I was comedy, and lesbians were not funny. The lesbian characters [in the 1960s] were either tragi-dramatic or sexy and therefore nude. My type was an affable, buttoned-down pseudo-intellectual.

BH: **You weren't given a girlfriend, on TV or in films.**

NK: The only lesbians with girlfriends were those in movie love scenes or nude scenes. Actually sex scenes.

BH: **When it's a heterosexual sex scene, it's called a love scene.**

NK: True. I did not do those. No, no. Always buttoned down, thank you. In fact, much of the mail I received during "The Beverly Hillbillies" was in the form of questions about financial advice or advice to the lovelorn. I was an agony aunt! [Chuckles.]

BH: **A tribute to Jane Hathaway's smarts and accessibility.**

NK: That's true. But I refrained from sending back advice....You inquired whether I enjoyed my work. What I hadn't grasped before being in Hollywood and acting at it was that one can't really shape one's destiny and development as a performer. For anyone in Hollywood, particularly an actress, her face is her fortune. Or her small fortune. A living, anyway. I once read a poem titled "The Actress." It said, "I can't say I enjoyed it, but the pay was good." I didn't feel that way all the time but...now and again.

BH: **You were first directed by George Cukor.**

NK: I thought I'd hit the jackpot. His film before ours was *Born Yesterday*, which won the Academy Award for Judy Holliday, who was a wondrous actress and comedienne.

BH: **Did you know she was lesbian or by?**

NK: I'd always heard she'd lived with a policewoman. But Mr. Cukor directed a number of actors in their Oscar-winning performances and discovered a lot of young talent and made several stars—Anthony Perkins, Aldo Ray, Judy Holliday, Jack Lemmon, myself....I had no misconceptions about myself or my role, but I believed it might lead to more than it actually did.

BH: **Your next time for Cukor, it was a bit role.**

NK: Oh, yes. Any illusions I'd had were scattered by then. I was trying to break into TV journalism to develop a career and have a steady income. It was a burgeoning field, however extremely competitive and extremely sexist.

BH: **There were no Barbara Walters yet.**

NK: No, it was dismal. Very disheartening.

BH: **You had a small part in *Sabrina*. How was Billy Wilder to work with?**

NK: Intelligent but not kindly. Mr. Cukor had more warmth. They could both be martinets, but I found Wilder sometimes liked to tear others down. I witnessed a few incidents, but I haven't made them public and still choose not to.

BH: **In *Sabrina*, Audrey Hepburn begins as a chauffeur's daughter but, Cinderella-like, marries into wealth. What was she like?**

NK: She seemed nice, and she would smile—some stars only smile for the camera. [Snickers.] But as with most stars, they're surrounded by their protecters, a retinue...and an aura or barrier that keeps lesser mortals away or in their place.

BH: **Hollywood is not a democratic place.**

NK: The caste system is alive and well. [Chuckles.] It's amusing, though actually it isn't. Theater is far more egalitarian, and of course in journalism, one can advance through one's own merits.

BH: Do you ever regret not having pursued journalism?

NK: What might have been? There would have been fewer restrictions on me, more steady work, but strangely enough, I've probably made more of myself, commercially, as an actor.

BH: Mentioning that word, why haven't we seen you in more TV commercials?

NK: They want a pretty actress to sell the product, young and pretty, or if one's a celebrity, one must usually be a *big* celebrity. That's when they hire actresses at all. Studies reveal that the public believes the sincerity of an actor more than it does that of an actress. Why, I cannot fathom. Men have created all of history's treaties, cease-fires, and other declarations and manifestos, and then broken almost every single one.

You referred to the Cinderella story, regarding *Sabrina*, but what one forgets is that it's a very sexist and unfair story or myth. Because the servant or poor girl can only win the hand or name of the prince if she is pretty enough to interest him. Her talent or kindness or intelligence doesn't signify; only her face.

BH: So many tales and legends treat beauty or good looks like a virtue. One that no successful woman can be without.

NK: Men wrote all those things, and the religions, too.

BH: Moving from ancient and medieval prejudices to modern ones: you were in the military. What drew you to it, and what moved you away from it?

NK: If I did write a book, this would be one of the longer chapters. I was attracted to it. One of the obvious reasons was patriotism. Another, the all-female atmosphere. Why I left....I felt it was a dead end. I didn't want to make a career of it. There was a constant, unspoken command that each of us had to play at the role, a contradictory role, given that by nature the armed forces are tough and aggressive. Yet we had to pay lip service to...things like lipstick and boyfriends and occasional ladylike mannerisms or statements.

BH: Do you think most women in the military are lesbian?

NK: One can never know the true percentage, and while it may or may not be a majority, it is a large percentage.

BH: What, a fourth or a third...?

NK: Very easily one-fourth, and possibly half, or most.

BH: And yet things don't improve because nobody in that large percentage speaks up and out.

NK: Not enough speak up. It's true. In the 1940s, I daresay no one spoke up.

BH: What prompted you to run for Congress?

NK: A desire to serve....This is a bit of a sore point with me. When I was running, I often got asked if I was doing it for the publicity? Or because I was washed up as an actor?

BH: That could also have been asked of George Murphy or Ronald Reagan. Or the guy who played "Gopher" on "The Love Boat"—he wasn't going to rise any higher than a supporting actor.

NK: Too true. And all the male actors you have mentioned were voted into office, and each was a Republican. The public prefers an angry actor.

BH: Can you briefly tell me how Buddy Ebsen helped you lose?

NK: He was no buddy to me. His real name is Christian Ebsen, and he has been a bitter man since losing the Tin Man in *The Wizard of Oz* [while making the 1939 film, Ebsen suffered metallic poisoning and was replaced by Jack Haley]. To cut the story short, there was a

"Beverly Hillbillies" reunion [TV] movie [in 1981]. All seemed well between Mr. Ebsen and myself, or at least as usual. His ego was even larger than Mr. Bailey's.

Then I ran for Congress, and next thing I hear, Ebsen, a Californian, is involved in our Pennsylvania politics, of which he knows nothing, and is making radio ads supporting my Republican opponent and claiming I'm too liberal for Pennsylvania—a Hollywood pinko, as it were! I was speechless at such a betrayal, and something so needless and cruel, such Gestapo tactics.

BH: And by the cruelty, betrayal, or stupidity of the voters?

NK: Yes, the majority of voters. The patriarchy won again—with the help of plenty of women voters—but it's over and done with, and I'd like not to talk about it further.

BH: What do you think of openly gay Congressman Barney Frank [the Democrat from Massachusetts's Fourth District]?

NK: I think he's terrific!

BH: So do I. A real hero, and an effective leader for all.

NK: I'm sure you know he was "outed" while in office. He's an example of a VIP who was outed and then decided to remain outside the closet, doing good for his own kind and others.

BH: Where do you stand on outing?

NK: Well, anyone can be outed, although we're talking about public figures, who are influential individuals with private yet public lives. But most figures who are outed deny it. Outing can only work if a Barney Frank says, "Yes, it's true. So what?" And then gets on with his life.

BH: And his new freedom. Had you been elected to Congress, might you someday have come out?

NK: Not in office. Not voluntarily. If I were outed, then I would not deny it. Although it would be wiser and more effective to come out as a politician than a performer, and I imagine that had I become a congresswoman, I wouldn't have acted after that—it would be anti-climactic. And I tell you why I wouldn't formally come out now: because the news and journalists would probably give it a pathetic angle—she's practically retired, hasn't worked in ages, her acting career is over, so she's saying it for publicity. I can imagine....Actors who speak up, whether it's about being different or trying to be taken seriously as a potential politician, are treated terribly. To add insult to injury, I fancy that they'd add something on the order of, "As if we didn't already know...or hadn't guessed years ago."

BH: It's not as dignified for older people as for, say, rock stars, is it?

NK: Coming out? No, it's not. If one is past fifty or sixty, it's almost like saying that most of your life you've been too embarrassed to admit it or to speak up.

BH: May I ask if your ex-husband was gay?

NK: You just did, but I'd rather not go into that.

BH: Or whether he's still alive or what he does?

NK: That's correct.

BH: What do you do in your spare time?

NK: I do keep busy. I live very much in the present, except when I read—then I can live in any place or time or body. And my ladies keep me busy too.

BH: Oh?

NK: My *dogs*. [Snickers.] A woman's best friends.

BH: Has there been—other than contractually—a Significant Other in your life?

NK: [Grins.] Into every life a little romance must fall.

BH: You know, you're a woman of mystery.

NK: I know. [Clucks contentedly.]

And so Jane Hathaway rescued Nancy Kulp from being a publicist and from non-responsive TV journalism, and delayed by several years the dead end of playing spinsters. Unlike the older Ebsen, Nancy did not, post-"Hillbillies," find a long-running replacement role, let alone her own series (Ebsen played veteran detective "Barnaby Jones"). But then, the time scales of actors and actresses are weighted differently; when Irene Ryan began playing the superannuated Granny, she was in her late fifties and only five years older than "Buddy"/Jed Clampett.

Besides running for Congress, Kulp served on the board of directors of the Screen Actors Guild, and was artist-in-residence at Juniata College in Huntingdon, Pennsylvania. In 1986 she directed Juniata's production of *The Time of Your Life* and was also a cast member, explaining, "When I set out to become an actor, I had no special impulse to do comedy. But people found my primness and features amusing, and now I'm acting for the pleasure of it, and teaching theater and film history. I suppose I've become a bit historic myself."

For two decades, Nancy divided her time between California, Pennsylvania, and Florida. During thirty-five or so years, she owned about forty houses. Real estate was her avocation, according to Paul Henning, who felt Kulp was "married to her career." Other associates also shed minimal light on the real Nancy Kulp. Robert Cummings cracked, "Nancy doesn't really talk about her past—maybe because she hasn't had one yet!" Irene Ryan, who had two husbands [one her vaudeville partner] and no offspring, apologized for Nancy, "She loves men, but she's darn choosy. She's waiting for the right knight in shining armor."

Actress Beverly Garland posthumously and cautiously stated, "She didn't like a lot of men, because she thought they weren't very bright, I think."

I learned of Nancy's cancer from our mutual friend, a lesbian bank examiner who'd been her lover in 1960 and '61 and thereafter remained a confidante. She'd declined to discuss Nancy or their relationship, preferring instead to arrange a 1989 interview at a Palm Springs Denny's restaurant where Nancy could converse with me on those subjects she approved.

During a sunny February in 1991, Nancy Kulp died at her home in Palm Desert, near Palm Springs. She was sixty-nine. The *Lesbian News* declared that she was the sole role model for young sixties' lesbians as Jane Hathaway, that she was "Miss Hathaway" to her boss and had everyone's respect and an orderly, contented life. Jane was even a member of the all-female Biddle's Bird-Watchers and "stood for every young lesbian's first crush."

Lily Tomlin, who played Miss Hathaway in Penelope Spheeris's 1993 "Beverly Hillbillies" feature film, also paid tribute to Kulp as a role model and pop culture icon — "a pre-feminist, pre-executive office heroine and can-do woman."

Nonthespians

DOROTHY ARZNER

(1 9 0 0 – 1 9 7 9)

She is the only Hollywood director of note who has never been biographed in book form. Dorothy Arzner was and still is the cinema's leading female director. Her last film was in 1943, *First Comes Courage*, a forgotten movie. It was taken away from her, and rather than fight Hollywood's entrenched sexism and homophobia, the retiring Arzner left feature films behind. Eventually she became a recluse in the desert.

Feminists rediscovered Arzner in the 1970s, and women's film studies underscored the female bonding in much of her work. In the 1920s, Arzner was considered one of the "Top Ten" directors, and she helmed Paramount's first talkie. She helped make stars of Clara Bow, Katharine Hepburn, and Rosalind Russell, and also worked with Lucille Ball, Merle Oberon, Sylvia Sidney, Anna Sten, and Joan Crawford.

99

(Arzner and Crawford were romantically linked, and a memorable photo shows the two dressed in the mannish suits—with skirts—that were Dorothy's trademark and which Louis B. Mayer abhorred.)

Although feminists reclaimed Arzner and thrust her, somewhat against her will, into a relative spotlight in the seventies, they deliberately overlooked her lesbianism, for it was a time when mainstream feminism was trying for an exclusively heterosexual image to offset the negativity and loathing directed at feminists by the establishment and media. Arzner was quite willing to shy away from such "controversial" topics as feminism and lesbianism. Since her death, her gayness has been frequently commented on in books about other tinseltown figures and in quotes from a wide range of stars and film makers.

Hollywood's greatest gay director, George Cukor, offered, "She was too tough for Hollywood. Most of her movies were hits, which is a track record Hollywood loves. But she didn't modify her ways or looks or manner. As a woman directing movies, she was looked on by most as a freak. And as *that* kind of woman, they found her less and less acceptable. They didn't want her inside their golden boys' club."

Arzner's directorial career began in 1927 and spanned seventeen films in as many years. She later expressed amazement that it had lasted that long.

Originally she wanted to be a doctor. But though born in San Francisco, she grew up in Los Angeles, where her father owned the Hoffman Cafe, popular with such movie heavyweights as D.W. Griffith, Charlie Chaplin, Mack Sennett, Erich Von Stroheim, and Hal Roach.

During the Great War, Dorothy drove an ambulance. She attended USC to pursue her medical studies, but siren celluloid beckoned, and she determined to have a career in film.

Behind the camera, for Arzner was boyish, robust, and not cosmetically inclined. Her goal was to help make and shape pictures; she moved toward it by informing William DeMille (Cecil's then better-known elder brother) that the only studio job she really wanted was typing his scripts.

Months later, she was employed at Paramount. Half a year after that, she was editing movies. In time, she ascended to chief editor. In one year she cut thirty-two motion pictures, among them Valentino's *Blood and Sand* (1922), for which she reportedly shot some of the exciting bullfight footage. Arzner also began to write scripts, and in 1923 wrote and edited — with director James Cruze because she was "just" a woman — the first great western, *The Covered Wagon*.

Her repeated requests to direct were laughed off until in 1927 she threatened to quit Paramount for Columbia. The studio bosses might have let Dorothy go, but for the support of executive B. P. Schulberg's progressive-minded wife. Arzner was assigned an "appropriate" project, *Fashions for Women*, and the next day newspapers headlined, à la Ripley's Believe It or Not, "Jesse Lasky Names Woman Director." Arzner brought the film in on time and under budget.

Subsequent titles included *Behind the Makeup, The Bride Wore Red, The Wild Party, Anybody's Woman, Merrily We Go to Hell, Nana, Theodora Goes Wild, Honor Among Lovers,* and *Dance, Girl, Dance,* with "lifelong bachelor" Maria Ouspenskaya (renowned for the Wolf Man movies) as a stern ballet instructor in mannish clothes named Basilova. The surname recalled actress-producer Alla Nazimova, one of Dorothy's lovers and part of a sapphic "sewing circle" that also counted several actresses, writers and Oscar Wilde's niece Dolly.

Fashions for Women won a British award and was the first prize-winning movie anywhere in the world directed by a woman. Arzner's 1929 hit *The Wild Party* — starring Clara

Bow—is, according to the book *Reel Women,* "probably the first film in America to deal with the subject of female bonding in a positive, affirming way. There is a heterosexual love affair, but it falls a quiet second to the female friendships." *Wild Party* apparently marked another first, for on the second day of shooting, Arzner requested her soundman to attach a fishpole to the microphone and follow the performers around for better sound. Thus, the first overhead mike or boom microphone.

In 1936 Arzner was one of the founders of the Directors Guild of America. Pulitzer Prize-winning playwright George Kelly—the gay uncle of Princess Grace—wrote, "Miss Arzner has given more to Hollywood than any other lady and more than most gentlemen. She was an innovative artist and craftsman. Yet she was wiped from the silver screen and remains uncredited in most reference books because of her emotional difference....Hollywood better tolerates a distaff director if first she ensconces herself, as did Arzner's successor Ida Lupino, as a more conventional actress and wife.

"The thought of a lady film maker is yet a queer concept in benighted movieland."

It was via director Robert Moore—best known for Neil Simon's *Murder By Death* and *Chapter Two*—that I landed a telephone interview with Dorothy Arzner in 1978. I'd have preferred an in-person session, but she almost never saw outsiders at her home near Palm Desert, California, and even arranging a phoner was an off-and-on process. However, there were no taboo questions, though a friend of Arzner's told a friend of Bob's who told me that Miss Arzner—she didn't care for the then-radical "Ms."—did not wish to be identified as a feminist or lesbian film maker, nor to be labeled an ex-director (I wasn't informed how she did identify or think of herself).

And she reserved the right to terminate the interview at any time. I'd have thought that was inherent in the process of speaking by telephone. I expected a gruff, cagey, and firmly closeted interviewee. Instead, she was soft-spoken and seemed careful and pensive. My mind pictured her as she was in the 1930s, a handsome, full-browed woman in her prime. On the phone, she sounded more like the confident but unassuming college instructor she became after the celluloid tarnished.

BH: **I believe you directed three silent movies?...Unlike several directors, you survived the transition from silence to sound. Why?**

DA: I was always concerned with the technical side of things, so the newer technology didn't throw me.

BH: **It's said you were the one who encouraged Paramount to follow Warners' lead and try talking pictures.**

DA: I may not have been the only one urging them to do it, but I may have been one of the most persistent advocates of sound.

BH: **You were a rather new director. Was that a factor in your survival?**

DA: It may have been a reason for more experienced directors and older ones who didn't make the transition. They were used to directing without sound, so they would lean towards postponing something new like that.

BH: **Were you always mechanically inclined?**

DA: I was.

BH: **Did you play with dolls or trucks or something else as a child?**

DA: [Slight laughter.] Just about everything except dolls.

BH: **In my research, I came upon a newspaper article from the 1930s that said "Hollywood's Only Woman Director Never Bellows Orders Herself." That was the headline. Do you recall that?**

DA: I think so. It likely said that men wouldn't allow or appreciate a woman giving orders. That that was why I was the only woman director in town.

BH: "Woman" is a noun, yet people will say woman director or woman doctor, when it should be female director, etc.

DA: "Female" is both a noun and an adjective.

BH: Of course, it would be better if they just said director and doctor, right?

DA: Correct. But you're right in your observation. They say male model, not man model, which sounds awkward. They don't seem to mind if woman doctor or lady doctor sounds awkward.

BH: You may not have bellowed orders, but I've seen photos of you using a megaphone on the set....

DA: To amplify my voice. I didn't want to shout.

BH: You didn't have one of those voices that carries?

DA: I sometimes wished I had. Like newspaper vendors — boys.

BH: Did you feel much pressure — more pressure than was put on a man — to deliver a hit movie?

DA: There was pressure to deliver on time and within budget, and the assumption that if it wasn't popular, it might be the last one.

BH: In various long-ago interviews, you made a point of stating that you weren't financially dependent on directing.

DA: I wasn't boasting about wealth. I was saying in a roundabout way that I wasn't prepared to stay in pictures if I had to cave in to demands and interference which I felt were unfair.

BH: May I read a quote? You told one Francine Parker, "My philosophy is that to be a director you cannot be subject to anyone, even the head of the studio. I threatened to quit each time I didn't get my way, but no one ever let me walk out."

DA: That's me, word for word. [Snickers.]

BH: **You were ahead of your time in terms of the power and respect you asked for as a director. Directors weren't celebrities then.**

DA: Not celebrities — hired help. I should have stuck around until the *auteur* phenomenon. [Chuckles.]

BH: **You were born too soon.**

DA: In a way, I was.

BH: **But someone had to be the first, and it was you. Do you think you were "difficult"? I mean, we know *they* were.**

DA: Sometimes I was. They often were. Thank you.

BH: **With your philosophy of directing, weren't you on an inevitable collision course with patriarchal Hollywood?**

DA: It was likely just a question of time and their exploiting the occasion.

BH: **You said no one ever let you walk out. Until Harry Cohn on *First Comes Courage*, that is....**

DA: That's right.

BH: **With only one week of filming to go?**

DA: Something like that.

BH: **The official reason was pneumonia or ill health?**

DA: Yah....Hollywood protects you until about five minutes after the door's slammed behind you.

BH: **Were you let go or did you walk out or...?**

DA: Nothing's that simple....The result was the same.

BH: **It was also Harry Cohn of Columbia who ended the directorial career of gay director James Whale. You were both replaced by Charles Vidor [Whale's last was titled, *They Dare Not Love*, 1941]....**

DA: [Pause.] He was a very good director. A real individualist.

BH: **British and flamboyant. And he dared live openly with another man—he wouldn't get a wife. Do you think it boiled down to that? [No response.] Or was he to some degree difficult or antagonistic?**

DA: I think the first set of circumstances did him in. How demanding he was, I don't know. It might have been a reason, but I'm doubtful. He did very well by Universal, commercially and artistically. He could have done the same for Columbia, which could have used him.

BH: **Don't you think that a gay director or female director was more vulnerable than a heterosexual male director who might have been more demanding or delivered fewer hits but was permitted to stay the course?**

DA: What I've heard for an awfully long time is that a woman has to be twice as good as a man to be regarded comparably. It's true for any minority group.

BH: **Including, still, women, who aren't a minority.**

DA: Yes, even more particularly in today's films. There are a few more women directors, but they haven't lasted as long as I did. They work less often. One money-loser, only one, and it's likely the end....Even the stars are all men. The few women in them—

BH: **Excuse me for interrupting with one of your own quotes. A few years back, you told the *New York Times*, "When men do put women in pictures, they make them so darned sappy, weeping all over the place, that it's disgusting."**

DA: I haven't had cause to revise my opinion. And you?

BH: **Sappy and weak. The fire and resistance of a Davis or a Hepburn, a Crawford or a Stanwyck are missing in most actresses. Mostly now, they're just girlfriends.**

DA: You haven't asked about censorship and the Code [the misogynistic and homophobic Code enforced for over a quarter century from 1934]. When I do speak with film students and scholars, they point out its shortcomings. Correctly. But most forget or don't realize that the Code at least forced women on screen to *do*.

BH: In other words, the girlfriends and the mistresses and even prostitutes had to go out and get careers?

DA: Just so. If women couldn't be depicted as erotic or use their charms to make a living, they had to get jobs and become career girls.

BH: But only until they married at fadeout.

DA: At fadeout, there had to be a man and woman, newly joined or about to be, with a future full of traditional gender roles.

BH: Patriarchy.

DA: Yes. No variations.

BH: And a future brimming with children.

DA: "Be fruitful and multiply." It was the corollary to the motion picture's message of encouraging male-female pairs.

BH: Notice how often in films then or now the villain is single, while the hero always has a girlfriend or wife.

DA: Both, lately. Also notice that any woman on her own is threatening or even villainous. If she is a villain, she must be extirpated.

BH: Extirpated?

DA: Destroyed.

BH: What a non-violent way of saying it! [Both chuckle.] In countless movies of the thirties and forties, the woman who's a threat—even if she's Bette Davis, who always put up a fight—is eventually neutralized by a man who proposes.

DA: He proposes, she says yes to his terms. It's submission.

BH: Have you read *The Female Eunuch* [by Australian feminist Germaine Greer]?

DA: No. But it's a thought-provoking title. It's often done to women.

BH: **They're castrated of their power and sexuality?**

DA: Even physically. Female circumcision in sub-Saharan [black] Africa is a tradition almost never described in our country.

BH: **It should be. Also the fact of slavery in Saudi Arabia— black slaves—and such facts as women there can't vote or drive.**

DA: In Saudi Arabia?

BH: **Yes. Did you mind never working with Bette Davis? She'd have been ideal for you.**

DA: I liked her screen persona. I never knew her as a person. You said her characters often put up a fight. That's what women loved her for. She was feisty, and it was a fantasy for them. Of course when she didn't give in, she was...bumped off. Got shot, typically.

BH: **No actress got shot more often than Bette Davis.**

DA: It's as if in the current pictures somebody declared that the battle of the sexes is over and that the men won. The women don't put up a fight anymore. They don't even fight a man's sexual advances, for their own sake.

BH: **Do you think this is a backlash against women's rights?**

DA: Whatever it is, the men who write the films are now allowed, or for all I know encouraged, to degrade the women on the screen.

BH: **And to trivialize them. Is it true you almost worked with Garbo? Can you describe the project?**

DA: It never took place. It was shelved....Louis B. Meyer was the deciding factor. It would have been done under [MGM wunderkind] Irving Thalberg, but he passed away.

BH: Do you think Mayer, who must have sensed Garbo's real sexuality and that of the women around her [i.e. screenwriters Salka Viertel and Mercedes De Acosta], wanted Garbo directed—and therefore supposedly controlled—by men only?

DA: Mayer knew that I was independent. Yes, he wanted Garbo directed by men. Men he could control.

BH: You were also set to direct Dietrich....

DA: She'd hoped to do a picture about war from a woman's point of view. War had broken out with Germany. The title would have been *Stepdaughters of War.*

BH: We think of Dietrich as such a clotheshorse and glamour queen. Did she want to transcend that?

DA: Yes, however, they wouldn't kill the goose who laid their golden eggs.

BH: Even when she was no longer box office, and older?

DA: They're always more likely to repeat a formula that's often or occasionally successful than to try something entirely new....Marlene was lucky enough, or unlucky, to stay beautiful throughout her career. She'll be the last to wither.

BH: Did you have a crush on her? [No reply.] So many women and men did and do.

DA: I think so. I agree.

BH: Were you assigned to direct so many actresses because of your gender?

DA: They would avoid me for westerns or action pictures. If it was a love story, then they thought of me. The studios' A-scripts often eluded me. I would be given an actress's first starring assignment—not quite an A-picture in terms of prestige, but unequivocally not a B-picture. If the actress became a star, they got someone else to direct her.

BH: Why?

DA: They wouldn't trust a woman with an A-1 budget.

BH: I read that for your first movie, you insisted on a big-budget project. Is that true?

DA: I let [executive and producer] Walter Wanger know that I would rather do an A-picture at Columbia, which was then a second-tier studio, than a B-picture at Paramount.

BH: So they were prepared to humor your desire to direct, but only with a minor project?

DA: I backed them into a corner. I wasn't about to do it their way. I had years of experience and results behind me. I didn't want to have to start all over again, at the bottom — where they might have kept me, out of bigotry.

BH: It's almost surprising to younger people that such an illustrious career as yours began with your being a secretary.

DA: Do set the record aright — I was a typewriter. Or a "typist" now. Scripts, on a typewriter. The machine was called a typewriter, so was the girl who used it. That one machine created more opportunities for women than any other I can think of.

BH: Is it true that before you, talkies would use stationary microphones, and the actors had to remain in place while reciting their lines?

DA: In that era, pictures were much closer to the stage. Locations, expansive movement, and so forth were the exception.

BH: Had you ever wanted to be an actress?

DA: I thought I would like the results of being an actress, the rewards. I never thought highly of what actresses continually have to go through.

BH: Is it true Clara Bow initially resisted being directed by a woman?

DA: That wasn't very exceptional. [Chuckles softly.] Clara was devoted to flirtations with men. In her opinion, the more men on the set, the merrier.

BH: **Do most actresses like to flirt with their director?**

DA: Sooner or later most do it, if only for the crew.

BH: **Or their own protection?**

DA: If she's not a big star, it is a farsighted tactic.

BH: **Why do you think so many films from the early 1930s are all but forgotten?**

DA: Well, motion pictures reached their maturity in the latter 1930s. In style, technology, and format. Early talkies are now often regarded as quaint or archaic. They were also shorter, closer to one hour, which makes them too short for television broadcast, even with the myriad commercials they pad them with.

BH: **Your movies have been revived at art houses, museums, and on campus, but are rarely seen on TV.**

DA: That's the way it is.

BH: **And it's not just the films. Various major stars of the early thirties are almost anonymous now. One of them whom you directed was Ruth Chatterton.**

DA: In *Anybody's Woman* [1930].

BH: **Your film together turned her into "The First Lady of the Screen." It was a very transitory title.**

DA: One never knows, at the time, who is going to endure and who isn't. Or why.

BH: **You boosted Rosalind Russell from supporting player to star.**

DA: I saw the star quality in her before anyone else did.

BH: **Might one reason be that she wasn't conventionally feminine? Some thought her a bit masculine.**

DA: I like masculine qualities in people....I could tell that she had substance.

BH: The vehicle with which you made Russell a star was *Craig's Wife*. Is it really your favorite of your films?

DA: It's as good as any of them. I found the relationships interesting. The wife and her husband, and even more significantly, the woman and her house.

BH: George Kelly won several awards for the play, *Craig's Wife*. I suppose partly because it warned women to value their husbands above materialism and even the biggest, most immaculate house?

DA: [Chuckles.] There is another psychological thread in that story. She doesn't trust men because her father abandoned her mother and his daughter when she was a child. She wants a perfect life, so that nothing can go wrong.

BH: She's a control freak.

DA: It's more evident in the remake [1950]. It was less subtle than my film [1936].

BH: The remake, *Harriet Craig*, was more woman-centered and star-centered, as the title implies. I think it's one of the most interesting things Joan Crawford ever did.

DA: Great acting.

BH: Wonderful characterization. Many people say she was really playing herself—as actresses tend to do once they're older and surer of themselves.

DA: Joan was a friend of mine, a good friend. [Firmly.]

BH: Post-Hollywood, you directed over fifty Pepsi commercials for her, didn't you?

DA: I had more control over them than I did with my pictures, not omitting the one I did with Joan [*The Bride Wore Red*, 1937].

BH: Why do you think *Bride* is less remembered than many other Joan Crawford movies?

DA: It has its following, but...I couldn't say. She did so many pictures. Most of the early ones are out of sight and out of mind. Film buffs think of Joan in 1940s pictures or some of her 1960s horror entries.

BH: **Like *What Ever Happened to Baby Jane*? Do you think there really was a big feud between Crawford and Davis?**

DA: Publicity, I think. Mostly publicity.

BH: **Hollywood publicity would rather have us believe that two stars hate each other than love each other, wouldn't it?**

DA: Miss Davis had no such desire for Joan. [By contrast, numerous books and individuals have since noted the bisexual Crawford's interest in Davis, during and long before *Baby Jane*.]

BH: **I didn't mean them in particular. Um, why do you think it's said that 1939 was the greatest year for Hollywood films?**

DA: I have my doubts as to any magic attaching to that year. Several good ones were made in 1939. There were some mediocre 1939 pictures, too. One was *The Day the Bookies Wept*. To name just one.

BH: **Which women in film do you admire?**

DA: I'd have to think too hard to come up with a logical answer.

BH: **Then what women out of film do you admire?**

DA: I admire women who lead. Leaders....Golda Meir, very much. I've also followed with interest the careers of two other Asian leaders—India's Indira Gandhi and Sirimavo Bandaranaike of Ceylon. These are the first three women to lead nations. Bandaranaike was the first.

BH: **And the least known. A Buddhist, a Hindu, and a Jew. Do you think the USA will ever have a female leader?**

DA: In which century? I cannot predict the future.

BH: What do you think of the word "gay" for someone who's primarily homosexual?

DA: I think it is preferable to "homosexual," because human beings are much more than sexual response. In that sense, "lesbian" will serve. "Gay" sounds a bit flippant.

BH: How about some of the older terms, like "Uranian"?

DA: I knew a man who often used that word, and his listeners often thought he meant Ukrainian.

BH: Do you think that homosexual women should be called lesbians or gay women? Although the latter sounds like a 1930s movie title.

DA: It does. [Chuckles.] I feel that the terminology isn't the key. Whatever term is used, outsiders' bigotry will result in animadversions.

BH: In criticism?

DA: Criticisms.

BH: It's more important what a group of people think of themselves than what they call themselves. But to call everyone a heterosexual or homosexual isn't right or correct.

DA: When a rape is committed, the newscast does not refer to the man as a heterosexual nor as a heterosexual rapist.

BH: No, yet if somewhere a woman shot her female companion, they'd call her an alleged lesbian murderer.

DA: Or murderess.

BH: Do you think Harry Cohn was the worst mogul?

DA: Louis B. Mayer was equally...the same caliber of man. He had more power, ergo he was worse. It's the degree of power.

BH: Do you agree that the major difference between a Hitler or Stalin and a fanatical TV evangelist is the amount of power they've been given?

DA: I would say so. It is a good point, that people give such men any power they have.

BH: **People and, nowadays, the media. Did you really have a clause in your Columbia contract saying you didn't have to attend meetings aboard Harry Cohn's yacht?**

DA: One of my contracts had a clause to that effect.

BH: **Would he have understood that it had to do with your presumably not wanting to mix work with socializing, or would he resent it because a woman didn't want to board his yacht?**

DA: It's likely he resented it all around. But I wasn't going to work under those conditions.

BH: **Do you think he took your film away out of revenge? [No reply.] Or what really happened?**

DA: The true reason I retired from Hollywood may forever remain a secret, and I'd rather it does.

BH: **All right. You discovered another big star of the 1930s, Sylvia Sidney...**

DA: *Merrily We Go to Hell* [1932] was her first starring role, and it was a very big success. You've probably not heard of it. Miss Sidney is at another plateau of her long career, in featured parts now....I saw that she was frail looking but had a lot of mettle. In most of her pictures, she suffered, and she survived.

BH: **She's been described as the prototypical "silently suffering Jewish actress," whatever that means.**

DA: People weren't open about their faith then.

BH: **Not if it wasn't the majority one. You also directed Katharine Hepburn in her first starring role.**

DA: I directed Hepburn in her first vehicle....I get asked about that picture [*Christopher Strong,* 1933] a lot. More often than I can comprehend. It's your turn now.

BH: Why, if it's about an aviatrix, as they still call a female flyer, is the movie titled after the male character she falls in love with?

DA: I didn't write it, but a male name was thought to have more widespread appeal. Unless the female lead was a famous star.

BH: Like Joan Crawford in *Johnny Guitar*. Westerns, a male genre. At least they called her Oscar winner *Mildred Pierce*.

DA: Joan's last picture [1970] was called *Trog*, after a caveman....Her death last year was a great loss; I lost a good girlfriend, and we all lost a woman who defined the word "star."

BH: I know. I was in Spain when it happened, in a tour group, and all the American women over forty reacted with disbelief that she had died.

DA: She was one of the few legends. Joan began in silent pictures, which most audiences aren't aware of.

BH: Yes. But back to *Christopher Strong*. Do you think it was intentional for Hepburn's character to seem so butch in the first part of the film, before she falls in love with the married man [Colin Clive] and then kills herself when he impregnates her? And do you think such a plot would hold up today?

DA: Zoe Akins wrote the script, and she was rather brazen in some of her themes. I think she wanted for the heroine to be very much surprised that she too could fall in love. I think also that Hepburn stamped her individuality on the part, making her seem aggressively independent and at that time shocking to some people.

BH: Many filmgoers found Hepburn an acquired taste. What about the plot, which starts out so hopefully and then descends into typical misogyny?

DA: I think the picture is remembered for Katharine Hepburn. It was not an outstanding success, but it's better known than some of my pictures that were, due to Hepburn and due to it being the first picture that she carried.

BH: **I understand there was some coolness between you on the set, and you each called each other "Miss."**

DA: That was not atypical of the times. "Miss" this and "Mister" that. American informality hadn't yet taken over from English manners and ways of speaking. After Miss Hepburn was reminded by the front office who was directing the picture, we got along quite well.

BH: **But you didn't socialize in the thirties and forties.**

DA: She had her circle of friends. I had mine.

BH: **What did you do after *First Comes Courage*?**

DA: I made training films for the Women's Army Corps during the war. I did television commercials — you've already referred to that. And I taught. I found that very pleasant.

BH: **You began the first film course at the Pasadena Playhouse?**

DA: Mmm. And I taught at the university, in Los Angeles. Then I retired.

BH: **In the fifties and sixties, did you ever think you'd be rediscovered?**

DA: I didn't give it much thought.

BH: **Why do you think Ida Lupino seems forever to be apologizing for having been a director?**

DA: [Laughs.] Well, she didn't set out to become one. I did. She was a prevailing actress who got into directing by default.

BH: **Why are directors who are women so quick to insist they don't really give orders to men? What do they fear — unpopularity?**

DA: That will change. It's most likely changed in Israel and India and Ceylon. The example of women in positions of authority will make men more used to sharing their power. The power that women had agreed to give them.

BH: **The monopoly is ending. May we briefly discuss another female director? She directed only two movies. One is *Maedchen in Uniform* [1931], the most famous lesbian-themed film.**

DA: Leontine Sagan. Very good picture. She was brought to Hollywood. You know the story? She had to flee Germany because of the Nazis. She directed a picture in England. She came to the United States, and here she wasn't given her promised assignment.

BH: **I heard that Mayer opposed the lesbian theme of *Maedchen* and the fact that it had no men in it.**

DA: Neither did the 1939 Metro-Goldwyn-Mayer picture, *The Women.*

BH: **Directed by a man [George Cukor]. Or did *Maedchen* have any men in it? I saw it so long ago. Did Sagan's Hollywood career, or career-that-never-was, fall victim to local homophobia?**

DA: I don't know the whole story. But that seems to be the crux of the matter. She made a name for herself in theater, however. I believe she went and founded the National Theatre of South Africa.

BH: **I hope I don't offend you by reading a quote from Leontine Sagan. She said, "What could Dorothy Arzner lose if she came out, in her retirement, and admitted to lesbianism?"**

DA: [Long pause.] I think our connection is bad.

BH: **I wouldn't say it's bad.**

DA: This is a good final question for you.

BH: I didn't mean to give offense. I just wondered what your response would be to her question.

DA: To her challenge, it sounds more like. But I too have a question—Has Miss Sagan ever "come out" herself?

BH: I don't know.

DA: I doubt she has. If I'm not mistaken, she had a husband. I never did that. So she's hardly in a position to give advice or issue challenges.

BH: If she is, or was [Sagan died in 1974], lesbian and did marry a man, you're right, she's not in a position....

DA: Especially publicly. It's rather shocking to me that she would address me indirectly and publicly.

BH: I understand you object to being called a feminist or lesbian director.

DA: I am not a director. I'm retired. And whatever I may have been in my private life, it didn't pertain to my work, at the time, in motion pictures. You wouldn't call a woman a Democrat director? I would not.

BH: I would call her a director who is a Democrat, a feminist— hopefully—and a lesbian.

DA: That makes more sense. But now you'll have to excuse me.

BH: I hope you'll excuse me. It's been a privilege, and thank you for your time.

DA: [Somewhat mollified.] Thank you for your interest.

EDITH HEAD

(1 8 9 7 – 1 9 8 1)

$\mathbf{A}$ famous graffito proclaimed, "Edith Head gives good wardrobe." The lady would not have been amused, for she was a confirmed prude. Her sense of humor was subtle enough to miss, and she once admitted, "I'm not the frivolous type. Gardening and collecting art are my only outside activities. Essentially, I keep my nose to the grindstone."

She also noted, "When you love your work, that's the most satisfying marriage of all, and the longest lasting."

Head's brilliant career yielded more than one thousand movie credits and earned her eight Academy Awards. She worked for nearly sixty years and was Hollywood's most prolific and famous costume designer. As for her private life, it was screened by a manner and façade which were intentionally severe. Yet for decades tinseltown buzzed about her true sexuality, which was camouflaged by two contractual marriages, the first of which she almost never discussed.

Elsa Lanchester, the wife of gay actor Charles Laughton, stated, "She wanted you to think she was born Edith Head. Her real surname was something like *Poser*...." People she worked with sometimes said they never got to know the real Edith Head or even her real emotions on any given day.

Anne Baxter was a friend of Edith and her husband of thirty-nine years, Wiard Boppo Ihnen, who died in 1979 at ninety-one (Head attended a charity fashion show the following day, but by all accounts, the two were best friends.) After Head's death, Baxter disclosed, "Edith was emotionally complex but kept it bottled up. At work, she seldom let her hair down.... Long ago, we attended a screening of a Joan Crawford movie, *Queen Bee*. During one of the more virulent scenes, Edith turned to me and whispered, 'I wish I could do that.'"

Head was herself a queen bee who reputedly discouraged young female talent that might have detracted from her status as the industry's leading female costume designer. She informed more than one aspirant, "Producers don't like to work with women." And during the 1970s she dismissed "women's libbers in pants" and contradicted herself by saying that she'd fought anti-female discrimination with hard work and persistence, and that she'd never encountered sexist discrimination.

Hollywood reporter and author Paul Rosenfield wrote, "Edith wasn't an egomaniac, but she did like being Numero Uno." He explained, "I corrected her one time and said she was Numero *Una* in the biz. She corrected me and said, 'No, I'm with the men. Don't rank me with the girls.' Edith was a terribly closeted, discreet lesbian who had little use for most women as individuals or associates."

Actress Joan Hackett put it another way: "Edith Head came from a generation that was so terrified, it was afraid to voice support for its own rights, even the right to vote. Never mind voicing support for fellow lesbians and gays, and forget about coming out of the closet! No way. Not in this life."

It may have been such fear, as much as her natural reserve, that kept Head apart from others in Hollywood. Edith rarely got "chumsy"—her word—with the army of actresses whom she dressed. "She kept her distance," said Baxter, who also got along with *All About Eve* co-star Bette Davis (one of Head's Oscars was for *Eve*). "I felt privileged to be taken into Edith's confidence. She didn't much care to socialize with performers and had her own reasons for keeping to herself. Being an only child and introverted, she was used to it.

"Apart from which, she preferred to keep her own tastes, habits, likes, and dislikes completely private."

According to Rosenfield, "Edith feigned indifference to stars, said they were just like ordinary people." Head enjoyed telling—and writing—about how Marlon Brando, in his pre-chunk prime, "walked into my office one day stark naked" and failed to impress her at all. Small wonder:

"Edith's final Academy Award was for *The Sting*," continued Rosenfield. "So she got to see Newman and Redford in their undies, or less. But it was the women stars, the beauties in bras and panties, that turned her on, so she developed a poker face and an aloof attitude to mask her true feelings. When work was over, Edith would climb into her mono-grammed Jeep and go home alone—solo.

"Or *sola*, though she'd prefer *solo*."

Home was Casa Ladera, an adobe hacienda in Coldwater Canyon previously owned by Bette Davis. One of Head's few female friends was Elizabeth Taylor, a frequent house guest. Head bequeathed her a Mexican coin necklace which

Elizabeth had particularly admired. Taylor called her "a star in her own right," and Davis declared that "Edith didn't get where she is today by not knowing how to play politics. She is not only a first-rate designer, she's a first-rate politician!"

Born in San Bernardino (most sources gave Los Angeles), Edith Claire Posener would later subtract a decade from her age, citing her birth year as 1907 and falsely claiming that her records had been destroyed by fire. Eventual biographies cited 1898 or 1899; the latest sources peg the year at 1897.

Charles Laughton, whom she clothed as Nero, revealed, "Edith cannot abide her middle name and doesn't use or admit to it, so I'll not be the one to divulge what it is." (He didn't explain how he'd found out what it was.)

Edith claimed her father was a peripatetic mining engineer and that she grew up throughout Mexico and the U.S. Southwest. "I think that influenced my love of art, seeing the Indian cultures and their wonderful art on both sides of the border." In truth, as a child Edith lost her father to divorce and grew up with her mother, nee Levy. When she remarried, Edith took her stepfather's name of Spare, later skimming past details about names, divorce, Jewish background, geography, or education. For instance, she asserted that she'd never attended grammar school, yet a yellowed diploma proves she was graduated from elementary school in Redding, a town in northern California not among the more exotic ones in southern California, Nevada and Mexico that she professed to have grown up in.

Head claimed that for the most part she'd been tutored at home, growing up separately from other kids. In fact, when her family moved to L.A., she had to be tutored in mathematics. Regardless, Edith Spare was a shy child who avoided others her own age. She preferred animals and said that one of her youth's companions was a burro whom she garbed in festive hats and draperies of her own design. Her first Hollywood assignment would be creating an ornamental waistband for an elephant.

"Animals have no secrets to keep from you," she once affirmed, "and they won't give away yours."

Edith's initial goal was teaching, and she obtained her master's in Romance languages at Stanford University. She taught Spanish and French in La Jolla, near the Mexican border, then transferred to a girls' school in Hollywood, but didn't care for either. She felt, "Adults are generally more appreciative of one's talents than are children." So she went back to school as an art student, telling insiders that she'd found teaching dull and "I wasn't patient enough with children."

At Los Angeles' Chouinard Art Institute, Edith may have met her shadowy first husband, Charles Head. Most biographical sources list only one husband, Wiard. Another notes a 1938 divorce. Unusually, Head's May, 1945, entry in the exhaustive *Current Biography* makes no mention of her having wed, giving the impression that she was still single (nor stating her birth names or year). Paul Rosenfield felt, "It's probably significant that Edith got divorced the same year [1938] that she achieved a position no other woman in Hollywood had before—chief of a movie studio's costume design department.

"By that point, she may have believed she didn't need a husband any longer."

Gossip columnist Joyce Haber wrote, "Miss Head's first husband is various things to various people. Depending on the informant, he was an alcoholic, a suicide, or both. Or 'just' a friend, or gay, or both. Or he never existed.

"Miss Head has always been in total control of her image, even her age....She can get away with lying about her age because she seems ageless...neither young nor old."

When young, Head looked and acted older than her years. But at Chouinard she took a reckless, rather juvenile, risk toward a more exciting future by "borrowing" costume sketches by her classmates and submitting them to Paramount's wardrobe department as samples of her own work. On the strength of the sketches' skill and variety, she was hired.

With MGM, Paramount was Hollywood's top studio. Head worked first as an assistant to chief designer Howard Greer in 1923, then for Travis Banton, who joined the studio in 1924 but was, by decade's end, the reigning designer at Paramount. T.B., as detractors called him, was the cinema's most celebrated designer after Metro's Adrian, who was more closetedly gay, and Jewish—he wed lesbian star Janet Gaynor at the studio's urging and eschewed his last name of Greenberg.

Adrian and Banton established high-gloss, all-frills, actress-y glamour as a celluloid staple in one lushly gowned screen extravaganza after another, i.e. Banton created all of Marlene Dietrich's Paramount costumes. For fourteen years, Edith Head worked in his shadow. Only Banton was entrusted with creating the costumes worn by such as Clara Bow, Pola Negri, Sylvia Sidney, Claudette Colbert, Kay Francis, Carole Lombard, Dietrich, and Mae West. In time, Head got to do the clothes for the supporting players, as opposed to animals and extras.

Edith wasn't a stand-out talent, and much later offered, "I could draw a little, but I could also borrow. So I survived. But never have I said I'm a great designer." She insisted that her biggest professional regret wasn't not designing for, say, Garbo—Adrian created most of her movie costumes—or for a particular epic but, rather, not being permitted by her studio to design for the Chicago Cubs.

Head's first big break after entering Paramount was similarly underhanded. While Banton was away—purportedly in Paris to copy from the French designers—she submitted her own designs to new star Mae West. At first, West was reluctant to be gowned by a "nobody," and a female at that. But she was so taken with the Gay Nineties sketches that the designing woman earned what is believed to be her first solo screen credit for *She Done Him Wrong* (1933). Mae also used Head's services for her two 1970s movie comebacks. Of the floor-length Western gowns, Head supposedly quipped, "They cover a multitude of shins." The line was also attributed to Mae herself.

When Travis Banton left Paramount in 1938 to open his own business (later working for Fox and Universal), Edith became head designer and stayed longer at that studio than anyone except founder Adolph Zukor. When her contract wasn't renewed in 1967, she moved to Universal, which was glad to inherit her famous name as well as her by-then-indisputable talent. Edith Head's posh bungalow, dominated by her bevy of gleaming Oscars—"the men in my life," she half-jokingly dubbed them—was a featured stop on the studio's tour.

(The Academy Awards were for *The Heiress, Samson and Delilah, All About Eve, A Place in the Sun, Roman Holiday, Sabrina, The Facts of Life,* and *The Sting.*)

In the 1930s, forties and early fifties, Head launched numerous fashion trends. Among them the sarong she created in 1936 for Dorothy Lamour that was taken up by movie-going women as the latest in tropical swimwear. In 1941 her Latin Look for Barbara Stanwyck in *The Lady Eve* was a commercial hit and timely, too, in keeping with the Good Neighbor Policy. In 1949 Head's peacock gown and train for Hedy Lamarr in *Samson and Delilah* generated a mountain of publicity but not many imitators. Not so the much-copied strapless evening dress worn by Elizabeth Taylor in *A Place in the Sun* in 1951.

In the mid-1950s, there was behind-the-scenes controversy when Head earned nominations and then awards for Audrey Hepburn vehicles on which she was the nominal designer. In fact, nearly all of the European star's personal and screen wardrobe was created by her friend, Parisian designer Hubert de Givenchy. Elsa Lanchester, who didn't get along with Edith (though Laughton did), noted, "There used to be Oscar nominations in black and white and in color, so that someone like Miss Head could win two prizes in one year, per category.

"She wasn't the sole winner every time. Two or three big designers might win for one film. On the Audrey Hepburn ones, I heard she didn't even do one complete dress per film. Givenchy did all the work, but Edith takes most of the credit....She'll take any job she can — she's worked for every studio, you know — and all the publicity she can muster."

With the fifties, prosperity waxed while glamour waned, and Edith Head took to the small screen, playing herself on Art Linkletter's *House Party* series. She became more famous than ever as the Dress Doctor, dispensing to housewives such fashion advice as, "If you have a large bust, don't put on clothes so tight you suggest a sausage."

Apart from costume designer, Head was an expensive personal stylist to female stars whose off-screen Look she coordinated. Clients included Dietrich, Ginger Rogers, Ingrid Bergman, Barbara Stanwyck, and Elizabeth Taylor, whose Oscar ceremonies gowns Edith engineered so as to display a maximum of jewels and cleavage. As her heyday ebbed, she also began to produce books, having long since begun writing fan magazine articles, and to design dress patterns for the masses, besides attending store openings for a fee and doing cameos in several films.

Marjorie Main

"Most of the time I played mothers. That's acting!"

Marjorie Main—the butcher half of *Ma & Pa Kettle*.

Never touch the stuff: Marjorie Main and James Whitmore.

Patsy Kelly (and Barbara Harris, Virginia Capers) in her last film,
North Avenue Irregulars (1978).

"I'm a dyke. So what? Big deal!"

Patsy Kelly — Tallulah Bankhead's lover, costar, and maid.

Patsy Kelly

Nancy Kulp (opposite Thelma Ritter) in her first film,
The Model and the Marriage Broker (1951).

Nancy Kulp

"I was a brain symbol, not a sex symbol"

Nancy Kulp—"The Beverly Hillbillies" spinster with a secret.

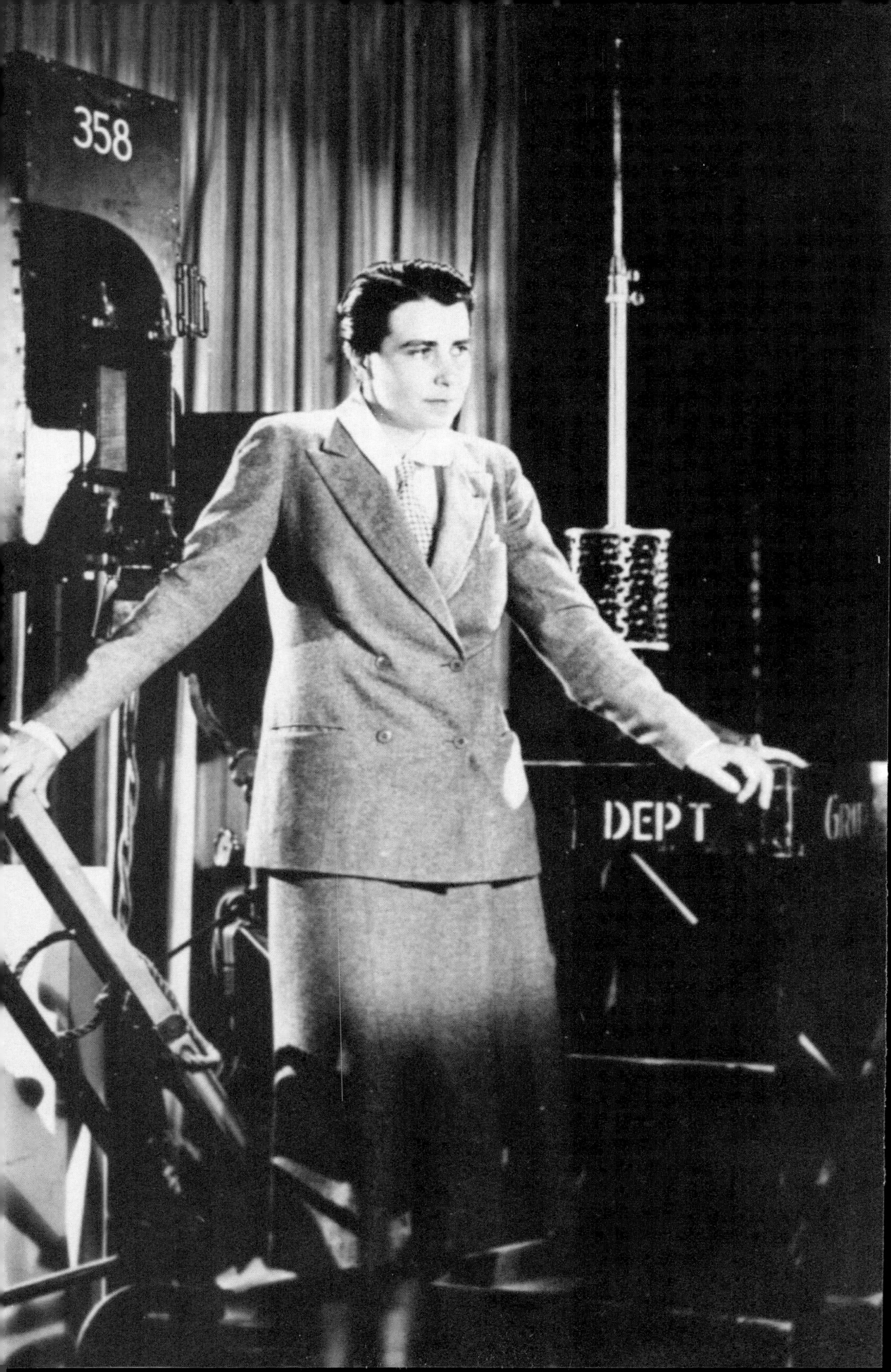
358
DEPT

Dorothy Arzner

"I like to think every director I've worked with has
fallen in love with me. I
know Dorothy Arzner did."

—Joan Crawford

Dorothy Arzner—butch, but unassuming; her nickname was
"Little Miss Mouse Fart."

Director Dorothy Arzner on the set.

"Edith Head gives good wardrobe."

—anonymous graffiti artist

The men in her life: Edith Head and six of her eight Oscars.

Edith Head

Designing woman
Edith Head.

Dame
Judith
Anderson

"I may play demons, but I've never played a wimp!"

Judith Anderson as Mrs. Danvers in *Rebecca* (1940).

Agnes Moorehead and Olivia De Havilland in *Hush . . . Hush, Sweet Charlotte* (1964).

Agnes Moorehead

"...one of the all-time Hollywood dykes."

— Paul Lynde

Agnes Moorehead — Golden Age "character star," aka
Endora on TV's "Bewitched."

Barbara Stanwyck

"My favorite American Lesbian."
—Clifton Webb

The Woman in Red (1935): Barbara Stanwyck acting with Gene Raymond.

**Born Ruby Stevens in Brooklyn, Stanwyck
became diamond-hard in Hollywood.**

Capucine and Hiram Keller in *Fellini Satyricon* (1969).

Capucine

"In *The Pink Panther,*
Capucine performed our love
scenes like a zombie."

—Peter Sellers

Capucine—the glacial French beauty was
rumored to be a transsexual!

Sandy Dennis

"Having an Academy Award lasts longer than sex."

Richard Burton considered Sandy Dennis "one of the most genuine eccentrics I know of."

The Fox (1967): Sandy Dennis and Keir Dullea argue for the affections of Anne Heywood.

"She was the first Hollywood designer to thrust herself into the public eye," said Paul Rosenfield. "Edith was in it for the long haul, she was going to drop at her desk, so to speak, and she knew the only way to become a celebrity, instead of just dressing celebs, was to develop her own highly publicized personality. She became a master at self-promotion, and though she didn't seem to, she basked in the limelight.

"This was contrary to the male Hollywood designers, whom the media preferred not to publicize anyway. Unlike Edith, most of them hadn't acquired a legal mate."

Meanwhile, Head's second husband had moved from art director of films like *Becky Sharp* (1935—the first all-color picture) and *Jane Eyre* (1944) to architect. The two were "close pals," opined Barbara Stanwyck. "Edith and Wiard don't socialize a lot or talk that much, but they love being together in their beautiful house." Stanwyck, no social butterfly herself, was a sometime friend to Head, growing closer after most of their associates had passed away.

Over the decades, Edith Head became a familiar if unexamined public figure and a symbol of Hollywood's gilded, once-glamorous past. Of her now-familiar Look, she stated, "When you're not a beauty, you have to create a trademark. I have the bangs, the bun, and the glasses....The teeth are from Barbara Stanwyck's dentist." Oddly, she still underrated her talent and insisted that her staying power was due to "knowing how to deal with the men in the front office. They rate highest....The actresses all want to be beautiful. I can help them achieve that, but the moguls and producers all want to be rich, and that's really in the public's hands."

Did Head prefer one type of costume, or one period, over another? She wouldn't say. Did she prefer a certain director or a particular studio or film genre? She wouldn't commit herself. A favorite actress? She guardedly declared that she did her best by all of them, eventually writing that the few she hadn't really enjoyed working with included Claudette Colbert, Paulette Goddard, and Hedy Lamarr. Had she any screen-writing or directorial ambitions along the way? She shrugged off such questions and declined to discuss film making or her work process in detail, noting concisely, "All I need is a script about a girl who isn't poor and doesn't hate clothes."

I knew Edith Head was supposed to be a lousy interview when I tried to reach her in the late seventies. Thrice I'd interviewed Mae West and had a notion of someday doing a biography of the fascinatin' and thus-far unbiographed—except, mythically, by herself—old West. Head had costumed her in her bizarre celluloid swan songs.

First I contacted Whitney Stine, a biographer and friend of Bette Davis, who would eulogize Head: "A queen has left us....She will never be replaced." Stine told me, "She might be willing to talk about other lesbians but not herself. She may not even let you get the *word* out before ending the interview." He made inquiries for me, but Head wasn't "doing interviews at this time." Years later, Stine revealed that Head had checked with Mae West, who didn't want anybody she knew talking to any potential biographers.

I'd recently interviewed Elsa Lanchester, the acerbic and amusing eccentric best remembered as *The Bride of Frankenstein*. The Englishwoman pronounced, "Edith doesn't like most women. Not if they're not young and attractive. Of course you must *know* she doesn't like any men...that way. She and her husband lead separate lives. He's usually at his ranch....He was over fifty when she married him—most people call him Bill. They were good friends long before they tied the knot, and after...they were *still* good friends," she'd smirked.

It was Lanchester who first publicized the late Laughton's gayness, while poo-pooing any suggestion that hers might have been a "marriage of convenience" on both sides. Lanchester hadn't kept in touch with Head, but knew a retired seamstress who had, and gave me her phone number. The ex-seamstress readily gave me Edith's home number; a secretary informed me that I should send her mistress three letters of reference from "known persons" in the business, excluding the former seamstress! She seemed perfectly serious, so I gave up.

For a few weeks. Then I thought, wouldn't it be something if I did get three such letters? I'd *have* to be granted an interview. Only, I'd mention nothing about Mae West. Head was pretty old, and I knew she wasn't designing much for films lately and couldn't last forever. A candid interview would be a coup if I could get it. In 1979 I did, via Paul Rosenfield, legman and ghostwriter for columnist-novelist Joyce Haber and himself a *Los Angeles Times* contributor; Ronald Haver, film historian at the Los Angeles County Museum of Art and author of a book about the restored Cukor film *A Star Is Born*; and Robert La Vine, a costume designer for film and stage and at one point director of special projects for Paramount Pictures. La Vine told me:

"After Diana Vreeland let slip that Edith Head's mother was Jewish, I got up the nerve to ask about her decision how to worship. Since she's a rabid Catholic, I was surprised to hear about her mother. I asked if she'd been hard-pressed to choose. She said no, her mother had always encouraged her to do what was expedient and that she, Edith, liked to 'blend in.' I never thought of Edith as blending in...."

And so I was given Edith Head's home address, directions, and a date. Half an hour before leaving for Coldwater Canyon, I got a phone call telling me to meet Miss Head at the Beverly Wilshire Hotel instead. In conference room X, and "Please don't bring a tape-recorder, a camera, or a guest, and limit the interview to one hour. Please do not ask Miss Head about her personal life or about Cecil B. DeMille." DeMille?

In the big wallpapered room full of chairs and one table, we had coffees, and in the midst of a discreet sip, Edith Head reminded, "If any of this, the hot stuff, gets into print in my lifetime, you'll hear from my attorneys." She wasn't smiling, just casually fierce. I nodded. She looked around eighty, but formidable rather than grandmotherly. (I've yet to meet any old woman in Hollywood who is grandmotherly.) We had more than an hour — I wasn't going to say anything till one of us looked at our watch — and her manner alternated between frosty and amazed at certain questions and a barely suppressed hunger to talk.

At the conclusion, prior to a brisk handshake, she paid me her version of a compliment: "You don't ask many dumb questions, do you?"

We started with small talk — not much. The coffee was brought (she stared at the young man's uniform; I stared at her staring), then a few comments about Mae West's over-with movie career (much shaking of Edith's head), and then she sharply inquired, "What do you want me to tell you about?" I said I was hoping to learn more about behind the scenes (the hot stuff) than the glitz of stars and awards. More about the designers (I couldn't very well say, "about the real you").

As if casually, I observed, "It's funny how some professions are stereotyped in reality as well as in popular imagination. I mean, so many male designers are gay but not many female ones. While so many female gym teachers, or tennis players, are, yet few male ones...."

She cleared her throat, pursed her lips, then stared as if to admonish, looked around the room, and finally began to speak.

EH: ...There's not much I can really tell you. I know that Samuel Goldwyn had an art director named "Fegté." Ernest Fegté. Goldwyn used to call him *Faggoty.*

BH: On purpose, do you think?

EH: I don't know. To put him off-guard? I don't know.

BH: Did Fegté react negatively to that?

EH: What could he do? He was working for Goldwyn. It was a good job.

BH: I imagine it was worse for gay male costume designers than—

EH: [Interrupting.] I disagree. Most of the costume designers were homosexuals. It was tougher for any woman to try and make a name for herself.

BH: I meant that homophobia was more often directed at males in the industry than at females.

EH: I don't know whether Mr. Fegté was a homosexual. I only know what Mr. Goldwyn was said to have called him.

BH: Repeatedly?

EH: Yes....I believe Ernest Fegté won one Oscar—in the 1940s for *Frenchman's Creek.* Pirates, I believe.

BH: You've won eight Academy Awards....

EH: The men in my life, yes. [Suddenly shifts uncomfortably.] I am appalled when actors like George C. Scott or Marlon Brando disrespect the Academy Award. It is a tremendous honor.

BH: It's probably more consistently well-deserved in the costume design category. So often the acting Oscars are politically motivated, or even popularity contests.

EH: I don't know, but I would say that sometimes an old favorite might be given the award over a talented newcomer. I personally see nothing wrong with that.

BH: Sometimes it's the opposite, and a Grace Kelly wins over a Judy Garland, or Judy Holliday wins over Gloria Swanson in *Sunset Boulevard*.

EH: Anything is liable to happen....I appeared in a film called *The Oscar*.

BH: I've seen it. With Stephen Boyd and Elke Sommer.

EH: [Stiffly.] It had an all-star cast. I play myself when I agree to appear in a film.

BH: Did you ever want to be an actress?

EH: Any female who says no to that isn't telling the complete truth. Every girl has gone through wanting to be an actress—every girl since silent films began.

BH: You said "the complete truth." That must be the rarest one.

EH: [Stiffening.] What do you mean?

BH: Growing up in Santa Barbara and with several friends in the business, we've always heard that [costume designer] Irene was lesbian, or possibly bisexual. That her marriage to Cedric Gibbons's brother was arranged—and for that matter, that Gibbons [MGM's art director] was himself gay; I don't know about the brother.

EH: Is that most of what you've heard about Cedric?

BH: Well, no. He married Dolores Del Rio and supposedly discovered her one afternoon at poolside fondling Garbo's breasts. I knew Miss Del Rio through my grandfather. She admitted that prior to Gibbons, her first husband was gay. He later shot himself.

EH: Cedric Gibbons would never have shot himself!

BH: **No, but Irene jumped to her death from [the eleventh story of] a hotel in 1962. [She was born in 1901.]**

EH: [Silence.] I remember. It was the Knickerbocker Hotel. It had a sad history. Frances Farmer went through a bad spell there, and it's the place where D.W. Griffith passed away, alone.

BH: **One of the pioneers of motion pictures. Do you know if Irene was lesbian?**

EH: I don't discuss other people's private lives.

BH: **I know you don't discuss your stars and what you've seen in the dressing room. But I think by now it's common knowledge that Irene was gay. Or bi.**

EH: I do not invade anyone's privacy.

BH: **But that's like saying that if you admit X or Z is heterosexual, you're invading their privacy.**

EH: ...Irene was not a happy woman.

BH: **Why wasn't she happy?**

EH: I have no idea. Her husband's name was Eliot [spells the name]. Eliot Gibbons.

BH: **Doris Day, whom Irene dressed, is the sole source for the story that Irene killed herself because Gary Cooper, whom she allegedly loved, had died the year before. [Years later, Day would claim she had "no idea" that her three-time costar and friend Rock Hudson was gay.]**

EH: I don't know about that. Eliot was a screenwriter, I believe.

BH: **I've heard more than once that Irene [née Irene Lentz] was a lover of Marlene Dietrich's.**

EH: I have too, and it doesn't prove a thing.

BH: **Well, I've also heard that Tyrone Power was in love with Lana Turner, but that doesn't prove a thing. Though we know that he went both ways.**

EH: "Double-gaited," they used to call it.

BH: **Oh. Nowadays it's nicknamed "AC-DC."**

EH: I've heard that. The Knickerbocker Hotel, by the way, was right here in Hollywood. Not in New York. Everyone thinks it's New York because of the name. These facts should be checked; I once read that Irene took her life in New York City. From the hotel name, probably.

BH: **Exactly—facts are important. More than popular mythology.**

EH: I don't know much about the private Irene. I know she liked hunting and guns and the great outdoors. Deduce from that what you will. She also didn't stay terribly long at the studio before going freelance....She was a loner.

BH: **She was the second most famous female designer in Hollywood. A distant second. Among women, you get virtually all the spotlight. Why do you suppose?**

EH: I don't know. I've hung in there. I started early, and I do not intend to retire. En route, I've stood up for myself. I'm a team player, but I've also looked out for myself. I had to. It was a boys' club, when I came in.

BH: **In view of Hollywood's enduring homophobia, one imagines male film makers would be more comfortable working with an Edith Head than with a gay male designer of women's clothes....**

EH: You mean costumes.

BH: **Sorry.**

EH: Not always women's costumes. Irene did the wardrobe for Miss Dietrich in *Seven Sinners* [1940]. Beautiful gowns *and* a man's naval uniform.

BH: **Unforgettable. She sang "The Man's in the Navy" while wearing it. Wasn't she gorgeous?**

EH: She really was.

BH: **Both sexes found her irresistible, don't you think?**

EH: Well, she was...a goddess.

BH: **You had goddesses then—to paraphrase Norma Desmond. I mean, Hollywood had goddesses then.**

EH: We still have great beauties. It isn't quite the same.

BH: **Do you think it would be intimidating for a rather plain woman like Irene to have to work with some of the most beautiful women ever born?**

EH: We're talking about Irene, aren't we? [Sarcastically.]

BH: **She did work with Dietrich and Carole Lombard, Hedy Lamarr, Constance Bennett, and I assume Del Rio.**

EH: I heard Miss Del Rio helped discover her....I don't know what her personal demons were. I understand she drank rather heavily toward the end. Not that that's unusual in this business.

BH: **The business of show—showing commercially appealing surfaces.**

EH: Yes, beauty. You asked what it's like to work with very good-looking actresses, but it's rather like being a chef. You know that it's appealing, and it is tempting, but you work with it so much that it...you take it for granted, and you realize that you have a job to get done.

[Long pause.] A smart woman realizes just how good-looking she is or isn't, and if she's wise, she knows how to make the most of her looks. A nonactress can't be starry-eyed or foolish enough to think she can ever resemble Carole Lombard or Marlene Dietrich.

BH: **Besides, you deal with their personalities as much as their looks.**

EH: I'm glad you said that. It would be different, were I dressing a mannequin. I have to deal with some very demanding and oversized egos at times.

BH: There are very few actresses, of your hundreds, that you've admitted to not liking. Like Claudette Colbert.

EH: I have never said that I disliked her. I did not care that much for working with her. Sometimes. Do not print that I don't like her.

BH: It's quite telling that most male Paris designers and most in Hollywood don't bother to conceal their nature by marrying women, while several New York designers do....Why?

EH: Because we design for the studios, and they design for the American public. As well as for stores like Penney's and...upscale department stores.

BH: Is the American public less sophisticated than the European?

EH: If they were, they aren't now!

BH: But if Europeans are more accepting of gay designers...?

EH: They're more used to it.

BH: How long does it take to get used to?

EH: It took a long while for Hollywood to get used to my being a woman....Why did you ask about Irene?

BH: She seems a very interesting but relatively forgotten Hollywood figure.

EH: She is. It's too bad.

BH: Did you ever hear that she and her husband lived in separate states?

EH: Yes. But they lived in a married state, as well. I believe in it!

BH: So do I, and it shouldn't be up to the state or church to decide which relationships are more valid or loving than others and therefore more fit to be legalized.

EH: I agree with you there.

BH: Besides, you must agree that in Hollywood, particularly, so-called marriages are often undertaken for professional reasons, not just love or commitment.

EH: Some are, yes.

BH: **Charles Laughton and Elsa Lanchester....[No response.] You knew him, didn't you?**

EH: A great talent. A very nice man.

BH: **Was it widely known in Hollywood that he was gay?**

EH: Many people did know he was a homosexual.

BH: **He was homosexual. Do you know Elsa Lanchester at all?**

EH: I'm sure we've met. [Glaring.]

BH: **A change of pace. What is the most famous dress you ever designed?**

EH: [Brightens.] You tell me.

BH: **Gee....The black cocktail gown in *All About Eve*?**

EH: It was *brown*.

BH: **In a black-and-white film.**

EH: It has been copied often.

BH: **Even by Bette Davis impersonators!**

EH: [Smiles—the only time during the interview.] I have never intentionally designed for female impersonators. [However, the last film Head ever worked on, *Dead Men Don't Wear Plaid*, included an enlargement of a dress worn by Barbara Stanwyck in *Double Indemnity*, worn in the 1982 movie by Steve Martin in a blonde wig.]

BH: **Your peacock gown for Hedy Lamarr was also—**

EH: Let's not elaborate on that one.

BH: **Was she easy to work with?**

EH: She didn't like to work.

BH: **Lazy?**

EH: Sometimes.

BH: **She retired relatively early.**

EH: Some people retire. Others get retired.

BH: **Didn't DeMille direct *Samson and Delilah*?**

EH: I'm not going to talk about that old so-and-so. Not here. [See *Edith Head's Hollywood*, published posthumously; it's closeted about Edith but frank about hetero Hollywood, including DeMille.]

BH: My first memory of you is on "House Party." We lived in Michigan that year; my father taught at the university at Ann Arbor. I was in kindergarten, and my mother watched you faithfully.

EH: That's good to hear. You really remember "House Party"?

BH: I sort of recall the severity of some of your answers, when they asked what could be done to improve the looks of housewives in the audience.

EH: It was very challenging. You saw some of those women.

BH: What stands out most is the shocked look on one woman's face after you gave her your advice.

EH: If someone is looking for honest advice and wants to better herself, she had better be prepared for some criticism. I was never brutal.

BH: What was the most frequent fashion *faux-pas*?

EH: Large women in large prints. I had to be tactful, but I had to tell a woman with a large bust that wearing a gaudy hydrangea print was not flattering to her.

BH: I'll bet they were thrilled to get any advice from Edith Head.

EH: Between myself and Art Linkletter, literally, many of them were overcome. I could have been brutally frank, but I tried to use tact.

BH: A celebrity can get away with a lot.

EH: With the public, yes, not with the critics or advertisers, necessarily.

BH: Who do you admire a lot among women?

EH: The late Mrs. [Eleanor] Franklin Roosevelt. She wasn't merely in the White House, she was part of it. A vital part.

BH: What do you think of the way most First Ladies dress?

EH: I think they could use a little Hollywood glamour. Or a lot, depending. Mrs. Truman and Mrs. Eisenhower were seldom in the public eye. They were the opposite of fashion plates. I think the two latest First Ladies look quite good and dress rather well [Rosalynn Carter and Betty Ford].

BH: What about Pat Nixon?

EH: I think she always avoided public appearances. I don't think she's that interested in clothes, although she's quite nice-looking.

BH: What do you think of the [British] queen's clothes?

EH: Queen Elizabeth doesn't want to offend any of her subjects.

BH: You mean by being flamboyant?

EH: Yes. Or going hatless. [Hard to tell if Ms. Head was being wry.]

BH: It must be comparatively dull for you, today's actresses being so non-glamour-conscious.

EH: It can be.

BH: On the other hand, an actress like Bette Davis always went for being in character over being a fashion-plate.

EH: There is such a thing as a happy medium. Bette has integrity. Bette has glamour. What I tire of is the actress who won't accept glamour, period.

BH: Is there such a being?

EH: It's not just glamour, it's also good manners.

BH: If a woman's anti-glamour, why would she become an actress?

EH: Good manners are for other people. It's a form of decency. In years past, an actress would attend to details when she came in for a fitting. She wore gloves, a hat, all of it, and she often brought in a small entourage—not just a hairdresser or makeup artist...sometimes her own stylist or manicurist.

BH: **And nowadays?**

EH: She might show up with her psychiatrist or hash-supplier. Not really. But it is appalling. I don't mind that the little white gloves are gone, but....

BH: **But there's much less respect from the young?**

EH: Much less. Not only that, there is less respect for oneself. Personal modesty. [Suddenly stops.]

BH: **For instance?**

EH: ...Several actresses now show up at a fitting wearing blue jeans. With *no* underwear beneath. [Glares.]

BH: **That is disrespectful to the rest of you.**

EH: It's disgraceful! They don't care how anyone else might feel.

BH: **It might be distracting, too....**

EH: What? Oh. I don't know—I just do my work.

BH: **Tallulah Bankhead and Carmen Miranda were notorious for not wearing underwear on the set.**

EH: They were exceptions! And they made up for it in other ways. They had plenty of glamour and class. They were still very polite.

BH: **But nowadays?**

EH: It's all me-me-me.

BH: **Actresses have more power than ever. Actors even more so.**

EH: That's another thing. Everyone wants to direct, even actresses.

BH: **Mitchell Leisen was one costume designer who became a director. You worked with him?**

EH: You didn't work *with* Mitch, you worked *for* him—if you gave in to him. We were cordial, but we gave each other plenty of breathing space. He was at Paramount for quite a while.

BH: Vincente Minnelli also began in design.

EH: ...I never wanted to direct.

BH: Why not? You became boss of your own kingdom, as it were.

EH: I wouldn't feel comfortable giving orders to men.

BH: It just occurred to me. Somewhere I read that Irene was waltzing partner to Walter Plunkett, who was another of the legendary Hollywood designers.

EH: Are you asking if he was a homosexual?

BH: No. It's well known he was gay. But it's interesting that, once again, a gay man and a lesbian will pair off, though platonically, and the public assumes each is heterosexual.

EH: [Sharply.] What do you mean "once again"?

BH: Well,...Charles Laughton and Elsa Lanchester.

EH: Is she? [Interested.]

BH: Actually, I don't know. Some close friends believe she is, and Laughton's brother said so. It's not easy to know if someone is one way or the other. Especially with socially induced denials.

EH: No one will admit it, so don't even ask.

BH: Walter Plunkett did the costumes for *Gone With The Wind*, to name his most famous film—and Hollywood's. Why isn't he more of a household name?

EH: You mean like Adrian?

BH: Yes, Adrian who took a wife and produced a child.

EH: That made for better publicity. So there's your answer.

BH: Yes, he was more acceptable to the publicists.

EH: One thing you forget. Adrian worked for MGM. Everyone free-lances now and then—most do—but when a designer isn't affiliated long-term with a studio, he has to fend for himself more.

BH: Plunkett was at RKO for some time, though. He did various Katharine Hepburn films. They were good friends. Platonic, of course.

EH: [Winces.]...I think he just didn't court publicity. I know he wasn't one to push....Oh! Walter's still alive. [He died in 1982.] Please don't print his secret.

BH: **I doubt it's a secret. I mean, don't worry. He's retired, it wouldn't hurt him—he's earned his spot in Hollywood history. But I doubt he'd care that much. I know he used to bring his companion onto the set, in the 1940s, and both men would sit there knitting.**

EH: That is astounding.

BH: **It is. I never knew any man who could knit....Tell me, what do you think of Joan Baez saying she's bisexual?**

EH: It doesn't concern me at all.

BH: **Nor me, but I applaud her openness and courage. Don't you?**

EH: It's very open. Wide open.

BH: **It also takes courage.**

EH: It won't cost her her career. Don't think that.

BH: **No, it'll cost her some bigoted fans. Fortunately she's a folk singer, not a choir singer. It's still quite brave.**

EH: People are shocked, naturally. But not so much about two girls.

BH: **But she's the first female celebrity to admit this.**

EH: That's not what I meant. All that pornography they make for normal men, it always has two girls together. In a sex scene.

BH: **Oh?**

EH: So I've heard [quickly].

BH: **Ah. What was Omar Kiam's real name?**

EH: The poet?

BH: **The Hollywood designer.**

EH: Frankly, I'm not feeling very inclined to dig up my old colleagues for speculation.

BH: **My curiosity was about his name. I'm sure he wasn't born Omar Kiam. Few in Hollywood are.**

EH: Do you know what Louis Mayer called Irene? He called her, so I've been told, Miss Don't-Melt-Ice-Cube.

BH: **Was that his way of saying she was frigid toward him?**

EH: I'm just repeating something. I shouldn't.

BH: **No, that's interesting. I meant that a woman called frigid often is called that by a man she wouldn't cooperate with—you know....**

EH: She had quite a deep voice, I remember.

BH: **Who are—without speculation; I already said that most female designers are heterosexual—the other famous women of Hollywood costume design?**

EH: Have you heard of Helen Rose? Irene Sharaff? I'm glad you've heard of them. What's your next question?

BH: **Looking back at Howard Greer and especially Travis Banton, whom you worked under—**

EH: [Not smiling.] But not literally.

BH: **No, but each one was the boss. Looking back now, how do you think of them?**

EH: As teachers. My teachers.

BH: **Did you ever envy or resent them?**

EH: ...Let's not talk about designers.

BH: **Did any actress ever proposition you?**

EH: ...Yes. [Stares me down.]

BH: **You weren't offended, were you?**

EH: Flattered. She wasn't crude about it.

BH: **What do you think of miniskirts?**

EH: You're talking the 1960s now. I made my view known at that time. They're horrendous. Most women's legs are not suited to be exposed by miniskirts.

BH: **Nice pun....Is it the lack of modesty you object to or women's legs, really?**

EH: Both. But most women's legs, above the knee, are not worth baring.

BH: **Even in Hollywood?**

EH: If you want to banish mystery and allure, put everyone in miniskirts. I don't do it. Very few actresses can carry it off.

BH: **Dietrich had great legs. Still does.**

EH: The legs, but not the vulgarity.

BH: **Who can wear a miniskirt and look good?**

EH: Shirley MacLaine. Few others. With Shirley, it's not really vulgar.

BH: **Do you find the extensive cleavage in the James Bond movies vulgar or appealing or...?**

EH: I love bosoms, but it also depends on what the woman is wearing and how she's behaving herself.

BH: **Usually preparing to have sex with 007.**

EH: That's rather disgusting.

BH: **I've heard conflicting information—that your first husband was a Chouinard student or that he was the brother of one of your classmates.**

EH: [No reaction.] You may ask a few more questions.

BH: **Is it true that there were no Oscars given for best costume design till after the war?**

EH: 1948.

BH: **Why did it take so long?**

EH: People often get overlooked if they're not on the screen.

BH: **Well, you made sure you didn't [admiringly; no reaction]. But not only people offscreen. Supporting performers weren't recognized until 1936.**

EH: How do you know the year?

BH: **Because the first Best Supporting Actress was Gale Sondergaard, a family friend. And a victim of blacklisting....**

EH: What is the next question?

BH: **Well, in the old days, a scandal could destroy a career. Or send someone into exile, like Ingrid Bergman. Don't you think it's healthier that today it takes more than a preg-**

nancy out of wedlock or being politically liberal to damage a star?

EH: ...Yes. I do. As long as actors don't exploit such tolerance.

BH: How? By being too pregnant or too liberal?

EH: Yes.

BH: Really?...There must be much gossip in the wardrobe department about the stars' bodies and shapes.

EH: And sizes. Not all leading ladies are created equal.

BH: So a lot of padding goes on?

EH: As they say, there's gold in them thar hills.

BH: Mountains out of molehills.

EH: But we never tell. It doesn't leave the fitting room. Not on my part, at least. I've seen most of the stars naked. Some are rather thrilling—beautiful breasts, bodies. There's no vulgarity in nudity.

BH: Naked actresses.

EH: Naturally. Who wants to see the men?

BH: Don't you think it's great that women are less hung up about their bodies now?

EH: No. I don't even believe it's true. They're just more immodest.

BH: They're more comfortable about natural functions. In the fifties, they couldn't even say "pregnant" on "I Love Lucy."

EH: Who wants to hear it that often?

BH: Young women are more...

EH: The most infuriating thing is having to sit through one of those TV commercials for feminine products while a man is in the same room!

BH: Yet you don't think today's women—I'm sorry—young women—are less embarrassed about their bodies?

EH: If you mean nudity, that proves my point about immodesty. Many of them think nothing of dropping their drawers in front of a man. In the old days, a lady wouldn't disrobe except in front of her husband.

BH: And even then, right?

EH: Right!

BH: It's sad and ironic that women have more comfort with and control over their own bodies in general, but not when it comes to feeling okay about their natural weight.

EH: It is sad. And it is ridiculous. The last time I was in a restaurant, I asked the waitress—a young girl—about dessert. I told her she was fortunate to look nice enough not to have to worry about eating dessert whenever she wanted to. I thought she was being humorous when she said that she's afraid even to *look* at dessert. She wasn't being humorous.

BH: Poor thing. Where does this come from?

EH: You're asking the wrong generation.

BH: You don't worry about eating dessert, surely?

EH: I do what I want.

BH: Good for you. Are stars much more vain than average people, do you think?

EH: People are people the world over. But stars are typically more attractive people and more neurotic.

BH: Why more neurotic?

EH: Because of...several reasons. This business makes them neurotic. They play everyone but themselves on the screen. Even though they're very attractive, when your face is seen up close on an enormous screen, you become obsessed with the most minor detail. And stars are paid so much money and attention and praise that they can't very well stay humble.

BH: Except in public. I've heard you didn't much like Paulette Goddard.

EH: I didn't very much like—and mark my words, please—her attitude. Any star should behave like a lady. If she's really a star, a true star, then we all know it. Any star should have some tact, but Paulette would come in and flash her jewelry collection in the faces of my women who were working very hard to earn a pittance of a salary. That doesn't endear a star to anyone. Next question.

BH: **Bob Mackie worked for you, didn't he?**

EH: That was long ago.

BH: **Unlike most who did, he went on to major success.**

EH: He's done well for himself in television. [Dourly.] What do you want to know about him? Well, never mind. Next question.

BH: **I wasn't going to ask that. Don't need to. Please don't get upset, but it's been said you were fired from "The Judy Garland Show" [on TV in the early sixties]. Is that true, and why?**

EH: [Long pause.] I left because I saw Judy in a certain way. I saw her in certain colors. She was by then a classic, and I wanted to dress her as a classic. The powers that be wanted her in more mod-ish colors. They didn't know what they wanted. First they wanted her looking very formal. Television is not a formal showcase. Or they wanted her too young. She was around forty, which they thought was frighteningly old. [Shrugs contemptuously.]

BH: **Is it true you were replaced by Bob Mackie and his partner Ray Aghayan?**

EH: You can do your homework and find out.

BH: **We'll switch tracks. Often, a masculine woman may be basically heterosexual, like...Ethel Merman. While sometimes a lesbian actress is quite feminine, like...**

EH: I know who you mean. [She did if it was Merman's Broadway rival, Mary Martin.] Go on.

BH: I'm curious who you, as an expert on actresses, think of as notably masculine, quote-unquote, and why.

EH: The why usually speaks for itself. I'll tell you as a movie-goer only.

BH: Fine. As a moviegoer, who do you think are among the more "masculine" actresses?

EH: I don't know....I didn't particularly care for Beatrice Arthur as "Maude."

BH: Why not?

EH: She was always trying to run the household. I felt sorry for the husband [Bill Macy].

BH: I always watched "Maude" and got the impression she was trying to stick up for her rights. She and her husband were both pretty argumentative. Who else?

EH: You yourself mentioned Ethel Merman. I like her voice. Her singing voice.

BH: And what movie actresses?

EH: Rosalind Russell, God rest her soul, played several busi-nesswomen in the 1940s. She had the genre almost to herself. She looked much better later on, as *Auntie Mame* [on stage and in the 1958 film]. Orry-Kelly did some wonderful costumes for her.

BH: Yes, and many of Bette Davis's Warner Brothers movie costumes. I know an author named Whitney Stine who was the ghost writer on Orry-Kelly's memoirs, which were to be titled *Women I've Undressed.*

EH: Not a very tasteful title.

BH: Nor appropriate. But it was never published. The design-er died before the book's completion.

EH: I heard that it had some revelations which couldn't have been legally published, at least in those days [O-K. died in 1964].

BH: I've heard that Orry-Kelly and Cary Grant were room-mates in New York, before they came to Hollywood.

EH: Oh, really? [Trying not to seem interested.]

BH: **More than roommates, actually.**

EH: [Disapproving glare.] Well, another actress who gives the impression of being...somewhat boyish is that English one...Glenda Jackson.

BH: **Very talented. Marvelous voice.**

EH: Very talented, but why has she chosen to go topless in so many of her roles? It's unwarranted.

BH: **There is a double standard when it comes to screen nudity. One rarely sees a man from any angle.**

EH: Thank goodness for that. I'm not narrow-minded, but we did get along for years without any nudity, and we had better plots, too. More romance. It was romantic then, not raw.

BH: **Which other actresses might be deemed boyish or even butch?**

EH: Mercedes McCambridge. Do you know of her?

BH: ***Johnny Guitar, A Touch of Evil* in an apparently male role, and more recently *The Exorcist* [as the devil's voice].**

EH: A horrid movie. Disgusting! Miss McCambridge must be in desperate straits, or Hollywood must be, if that's the best they can offer her. It's quite a comedown. She won an Academy Award [for the supporting role of a "spinster" in love with her male boss] in *All the President's Men*.

BH: **That sounds like a good title for a Hollywood novel, *Desperate Straights*. With or without a coast. But she won her Oscar for *All the King's Men* [1949], didn't she?**

EH: [Exclaims to the ceiling.] Oh! You're right—*All the King's Men*, not *All the President's Men*. [Shakes head.] I wouldn't read that book—the newer one.

BH: Are you...?

EH: No political questions.

BH: Fine. Who else was pretty butch, and sometimes they are pretty, like Jodie Foster....

EH: [A warning finger.] She's just a teenager, and we're not passing judgments here.

BH: We're not passing judgments.

EH: Don't be impertinent. All right....There was an actress, more of a stage actress, though she was very big at Metro in the beginning [the 1920s]. Her name was Alla Nazimova, and she was both a woman's woman and...rather masculine, all right.

BH: I've read about her. A fascinating personality. A woman's woman, you said?

EH: Yes. A lesbian.

BH: Why is there more obesity today? You've been trim all your life.

EH: I'm also short. Short and fat is the deadliest combination.

BH: Fashion-wise?

EH: Yes. People earn more today. Not everyone in the Depression could afford to become fat.

BH: But I go to other countries, affluent ones, too, and there's less overweight to be seen.

EH: We Americans are too comfortable. We're spoiled. Backbone is the real endangered species here.

BH: But are people supposed to get uncomfortable, or...?

EH: I don't like skinny women. But there's no need for fat. It's a sign of disrespect for oneself and for those who have to look at them.

BH: Some people don't care how they look.

EH: Well, women should. Ladies should care.

BH: Why should they care more than men or gents?

EH: If they don't care, I don't care. Never mind.

BH: Why do you imagine so many lesbians want to have children? And do.

EH: I have no idea. The next question.

BH: A very large number of Hollywood actresses never had children, even though they usually did marry.

EH: It doesn't mean they were sexually abnormal.

BH: In Hollywood it doesn't. But why, especially at a time when large families—tribes, even—were the norm, did so many actresses not have kids?

EH: Because actresses have to be vain. Some fear childbirth because they might lose their figures. Others, back then, couldn't—too many [illegal] abortions. Some went ahead and adopted.

BH: Like Joan Crawford.

EH: Don't get me started on that book [*Mommie Dearest*].

BH: Or Barbara Stanwyck. I hear she hasn't spoken to her adopted son since the 1950s. Is that true?

EH: And some actresses from Europe who weren't that interested in men weren't interested in having a child, either.

BH: Such as?

EH: You know the names, I'm sure....

BH: Garbo, Pola Negri. Hepburn...?

EH: I didn't say a word about Katharine Hepburn! And neither will you! Strike her name. She would sue if it got out.

BH: I doubt that very much. Anyway, I meant Audrey Hepburn—but, uh, she's the mother of two and heterosexual. Sorry.

EH: I hope you weren't trying to trick me....I don't think of Audrey Hepburn as European. Not anymore.

BH: She was my favorite star, growing up.

EH: You're not old enough to...

BH: **I meant when I was growing up. Where were we?...Pola Negri. I know she retired around talkies, but is she still alive?**

EH: I'm sure she is, though she must be around ninety. I hear she has a home in Santa Fe.

BH: **Truman Capote refers to Santa Fe as the lesbian capital of America.**

EH: Just don't print anything about her in either of our lifetimes. She denies everything.

BH: **Except having had an affair with Hitler. Can you believe it? Too ashamed to say she's gay or bi, but ready to admit an affair with that devil.**

EH: I don't even think she was a bisexual. Not the way I heard it.

BH: **"Was"?**

EH: At her age, I certainly hope she is asexual.

BH: **Oh. Well, ninetyish is late enough to stop, I imagine.**

EH: I read her memoirs a few years ago. [Leans forward, the only time.] It was titled *Memoirs of a Star.* Lies — start to finish. Very clever book. [Leans back.]

BH: **Somewhere I heard that she got herself a rich sugar mommy. Long ago, already.**

EH: I've said all I'm saying. Read the book. The other woman is in there, but not the way you describe her.

BH: **As you said, a work of semifiction. You know, there's one Polish joke I think is rather clever. The one about the Polish lesbian — she likes *men.* Isn't Pola Negri [she died in 1987] Polish?**

EH: Yes. [Not getting it.] She did retire long ago, but in the 1960s she made one comeback to the screen.

BH: **As what, Eva Braun?**

EH: It starred Hayley Mills. I don't remember [Disney's *The Moon-Spinners*, 1963].

BH: Don't you think Barbara Stanwyck has a pretty butch image?

EH: No, I don't!

BH: In her later films she does.

EH: Women have more character in their later years, that's all.

BH: I agree.

EH: Now let's end this list....I'll tell you who you should interview about this topic, if you're intent on pursuing it further. Two actresses. Patsy Kelly, the comedienne. She's known to be quite frank on some topics. And a younger actress, Joan Hackett. She smokes a pipe, she's a women's libber, but I'm not saying I know a thing about her personal life. However, she might give you some insights into all this, although she's too young to know about the old Hollywood—the real Hollywood.

BH: And you're not telling?

EH: [Rising.] As I already told you, I can't help you in this modern field of...research, only because I know so little about it. I've been around quite a long time, but I've worked all of that time. I did not stick my nose where it didn't belong, and if people gossiped, I didn't stop them.

BH: In one ear and out the other?

EH: No. I have a very good memory. I have enjoyed gossip from time to time. But it didn't go any further.

BH: There's gossip, and there's gossip. There's trivia, and there's history.

EH: I always felt, to paraphrase Harry Truman, "The buck stops here."

BH: No, you're quoting him exactly.

EH: Well, I meant that it didn't go any further, once I heard what people chose to tell me. "The buck stops here."

BH: Just so the truth doesn't. But I do thank you for your time and the insights.

EH: Are you going to send me a Xerox of your notes?

BH: You hadn't asked me to.

EH: I'm asking now. Will you send me Xeroxed copies of your notes?

BH: Don't worry. The buck stops here.

EH: I beg your pardon?

BH: I do agree to the terms we discussed.

EH: All right....I'm not paranoid or old-fashioned. But I do think it's very important, what people say.

BH: Yes, and what they don't say.

Dramatic
Actresses

JUDITH ANDERSON

(1 8 9 8 – 1 9 9 2)

Judith Anderson was the woman you loved to hate on screen. She was the diabolic Mrs. Danvers in *Rebecca* (1940), and a year later the lead in *Lady Scarface*. She played detestable or unloved characters in films like *Laura, And Then There Were None, The Strange Love of Martha Ivers, The Red House, The Furies, Salome, Cat On a Hot Tin Roof,* and *Macbeth* —her best role, said movie critics of her Lady Macbeth.

Her career spanned seventy-five years and dwelt upon the stage. An Australian-born British subject who moved to Santa Barbara, California, in 1950, she'd arrived in Hollywood in 1918. Her near-frightening features and manner caused her to be shunned by DeMille and other directors, and she never went before a camera till after the age of thirty. "In the cinema I acted seldom but menacingly." In the theater she also played the gripping roles that were her destiny. "People often think I'm going to do or say something terrible," she apprised the *Santa Barbara News-Press*, "but I rarely do terrible things...."

She began acting at seventeen and matured into her biggest hit yet, *Mourning Becomes Electra*, in 1932. Guthrie McClintic produced the 1934 play *Divided By Three*, with Anderson and Hedda Hopper. The gay husband of lesbian stage star Katharine "Kit" Cornell told gay critic Alec Woollcott, "Judith may never find someone manlier than herself to act with or engage."

The thespian's two brief marriages were topics she staunchly avoided. "After 1950 I never looked back or gave the institution a second thought." When Helen Hayes and Anita Loos coauthored a book that contained a passing reference to one of Judith's contractual mates, she was infuriated and thereafter professed a "hearty dislike" for stage rival Hayes. "I'm the only actress who's ever publicly disparaged Miss Hayes!"

Other memorable stage turns included her Gertrude to John Gielgud's Hamlet in 1936 and her acme as *Medea* in 1937, 1941, 1947, and 1949. She returned to the play in 1982 as the Nurse, opposite Zoe Caldwell's Medea. Maurice Evans, who played Macbeth to her Lady Macbeth, opined, "Judith is most believable when essaying a demonic catalyst of destruction." Her *Devil's Disciple* costar Eva Le Gallienne offered, "She cannot by temperament play wallflowers. Her talent would enable her to, but she thrives in the larger-than-life characters."

In 1960 she was created Dame of the British Empire — and appeared in a Jerry Lewis movie, *Cinderfella*. Ten years later, she made her screen comeback — in the Sioux language — as Buffalo Cow Head in *A Man Called Horse*. At eighty-five she signed on for her first film role in many years, in *Star Trek III* (1984). From 1984 to 1987 she played Minx on the soap opera

"Santa Barbara" at five thousand dollars a week. I interviewed the great Dame in my ex-hometown of Santa Barbara in 1990, soon after her ninety-second birthday. Within minutes of reaching her home, I was asked, "Do I look as old as I felt this morning?"

"You don't look a day over seventy-nine," I answered truthfully. I'd met her twice socially, years before, through visiting Scottish friends. She still seemed as intimidating and mercurial—one moment glaringly cranky, the next laughing heartily, head thrown back. Several locals swore Dame Judith had casually confessed her lesbianism—not bisexuality—to them or their friends. But our interview did not conclude with anything so self-secure or generous.

JA: I do hope you're going to ask some stimulating questions. Most interviewers I've put up with are weak as water.

BH: **What kind of question don't you get asked?**

JA: I don't get asked about the world. They think I'm too wrapped up in me as an actress or too old to know or care....What do I think of the Common Market?

BH: **What do you think of the Common Market?**

JA: I prefer to shop at Safeway. [Deadpan.]

BH: **Hmm. I love the answer you gave when some reporter asked you how being knighted—created Dame—had changed your life. You were rather flippant.**

JA: What did I say?

BH: **You said that you found yourself wearing gloves more often.**

JA: [Laughs.] I hadn't forgotten. I wanted to hear it again. It still sounds good. And it's true.

BH: **Few people think of you as Australian. Is that where you get your humor?**

JA: It's where I get....It's part of my hidden core.

BH: **You don't sound Australian.**

JA: I sound like an older Australian. We were more...bound to Great Britain. Culturally, and so forth.

BH: **Older American stars sounded semi-English thanks to studio vocal coaching. A Brooklyn or Southern accent was meant to be erased in those days. Where in Australia?**

JA: One of the loveliest parts, South Australia. The capital is Adelaide, where I was born.

BH: **An outpost of empire, right?**

JA: Yes, Australia was not yet independent.

BH: **And Victoria was still on the throne. Wow.**

JA: I did feel that "Dame Judith Anderson" was quite an honor.

BH: **Of course. Your most famous screen role was Mrs. Danvers, who famously urges Joan Fontaine to commit suicide. [She smiles gleefully.] In your most famous stage role, Medea, you killed your children. Were you drawn to violent characters, or did they seem more cruel through your talents?**

JA: [Laughs heartily.] You do well not to offend me! I appreciate the attempt. Is there a bitch behind the bitchy roles? That's what you want to know.

BH: **...Yes. [She doesn't reply, staring.] Or is it that your somewhat stark looks got you cast as dark-spirited women?**

JA: My face was the barricade to my talent. No matter. It's a mutual love-hate relationship I've had with film. I made a short in 1930. I did a feature [her first] in 1933, *Blood Money*, a violent title for you, nothing until 1940, and after *Rebecca*, which resulted in an Academy Award nomination for me, I did the title role in *Lady Scarface*. A B-movie, easily. Very violent, then.

BH: **Is it true Cecil B. DeMille somehow rejected you?**

JA: That was long before any of that, and the only way that overrated windbag rejected me was as a potential employer. He didn't employ actors, he used stars. He was the star of his spectacles or tried to be. Was easily the most over-publicized director in the business.

BH: **A pious hypocrite, by consensus. Edith Head didn't like him either.**

JA: Good! I always heard she trained to be a gymnast. She was very athletic when young. She's that type....But DeMille began as hot air and ended as hot air. Hitchcock became egotistical; DeMille was born that way.

BH: **You were in his final movie, *The Ten Commandments* [1956].**

JA: A remake of his best-known silent picture. He finally got it right.

BH: **Did it ever get depressing playing so many hated characters?**

JA: Oh, no. I loved it!

BH: **You don't shy away from controversy?**

JA: We all do, to some extent. I, not much, and the older I get, less so.

BH: **Quentin Crisp said about getting uppity with old age, "As it's toward the end of the run, one can overact appallingly."**

JA: [Claps, laughs.] Very relevant, very true. Is he an actor?

BH: **No more than most people.**

JA: Now, ask me these outrageous questions you promised. I hate dull interviews—reading them or doing them.

BH: **All right. I sometimes ask who is the most masculine actress...in your opinion?**

JA: That's a good one....Jane Wyman, in later years. Of course all actresses become somewhat more...masculinized with time. The aging process, and chemical... changes. Lily Tomlin, the comic, is like that already. And...Tyrone Power. Possibly. I don't know. But I like the question.

BH: **And its obverse—who is the most effeminate actress?**

JA: Oh, I like that! Most of them—when young. Loretta Young, when she was...I know: Zasu Pitts. The most effeminate of actresses. Very bovine. Rolling eyes and those endlessly fluttering hands. A very funny actress— for a minute or so. Who do you think is the most effeminate?

BH: **Katharine Hepburn, when she's trying to be all femme-y, especially opposite Spencer Tracy. Did you see *Desk Set* [1957]?**

JA: I did. Painful! I know what you mean.

BH: **One of my favorite Judith Anderson lines is from the 1945 version—the best, most agree—of Agatha Christie's *And Then There Were None*.**

JA: Did I say anything particularly vindictive in that one?

BH: **Well, the butler was murdered overnight, so next morning you said, "Very stupid to kill the only servant in the house. Now we don't even know where to find the marmalade."**

JA: [Laughs heartily, claps.] Marvelous! I feel sure if they'd had these idiotic Q-ratings for popularity, I would have been one of the least popular performers in the 1940s and 1950s. At least if I did my job well.

BH: **Did you ever wish for softer roles?**

JA: A softer face, more like. Softer roles—what for? [Dismissively flicks hand.] To play ordinary types? Everyday women?

BH: **This isn't flattery, but though you didn't often do movies, whenever you were in one, you made a lasting impression.**

JA: Friends and enemies alike say I was disturbing to people, in most of my roles.

BH: Do you have any, or many, enemies?

JA: Of course I do! The only people without enemies are anonymous ones.

BH: Here's a question to which the answer could be controversial. What woman or women do you admire?

JA: I am not a follower nor a worshipper. I stopped seeking leaders and models ages ago. We're all fallible. All so fragmented. I admit it, readily. I am frankly cantankerous, always was. Shows on my face. Most of the members of my gender aren't permitted to be the least bit cantankerous until they're old, divorced, or widowed. I never waited for anyone to give me permission to reveal what I felt. If I felt moody or angry, I damn well showed it!

BH: Present tense not excluded! [Both laugh.] Are there any women you do admire?

JA: I'll tell you who I don't admire, and I think it's daft placing them on those most-admired-women lists every year. That's the wives or widows of famous men.

BH: It is sexist. People of achievement should be admired, but what has a long-suffering wife, say, Mrs. Nixon, got that puts her on such a list, ahead of hundreds of women who have achieved something themselves?

JA: That's what I say! For years, Jackie Kennedy or Onassis is on the list. Because her husband died? Because she's still slim? Or has children? Why was Nancy Reagan on the list? Every First Lady is on the list, and Miss [Nancy] Davis was a decidedly unsuccessful actress. Who then married a mildly successful actor. Later, they were very lucky. And America was not.

BH: Do you want to share your political philosophy?

JA: Why should I? Politics bore the pants off people.

BH: **That's one way of keeping America beautiful.**

JA: [Doesn't laugh.] Another one—Mrs. Johnson. Lady Bird. Not the witch Nancy Reagan was, though she looked more like one. She got on that most-admired list for being her husband's wife. Mrs. First-Lady.

BH: **And for trying to keep America beautiful. I was a child, but I remember that.**

JA: I remember the joke. "Lady Bird is doing her bit to keep America beautiful. She just left the country."

BH: **She seems to have more spirit than most First Ladies, which when you think of it is not only a sexist term, but undemocratic. Like First Comrade or First Citizen.**

JA: No one is supposed to be first.

BH: **Or last. You haven't named any women you admire, so are there any professions you admire?**

JA: For women? Oh....I find it intriguing that only two professions permit a woman not to have to state her marital status at every turn—doctor and actress. Both healers, you see. The physician and the entertainer.

BH: **That's right. Legally you might be Miss or Mrs. Anderson, but as one you're Dr. Anderson—professors too—and as an actress it's Miss Anderson. Or Ms. Anderson.**

JA: I still think "Ms." sounds so Southern.

BH: **It's just what one's used to. But of course it's the idea of not labeling women by marital status, and only women.**

JA: I don't disagree, it's just the word they chose, whoever did choose "Ms."

BH: **Whatever the word, it's the concept that matters, and no one word will please everyone. And who chose "Miss" and "Mrs." or "Mr."? But that was long ago, so we're used to them.**

JA: I don't want to sound *too* agreeable, but I think the word "gay" fits. Most gay men I know *are* gay, in both meanings of the word. It's a short, easy word for men or women.

BH: **What about the word "lesbian"?**

JA: It's Greek to me.

BH: **It *is*.**

JA: I have a local acquaintance who is half my age and adores dogs, but she becomes upset whenever the word "gay" is used to mean homosexual. She always complains that they've ruined a perfectly good word.

BH: **I would say that 5 to 10 percent of the world's human beings are more important than any three-letter word in one language. Or all the words.**

JA: I don't argue with her. [Shrugs.]

BH: **I'm surprised....Who's the phoniest actress in Hollywood?**

JA: You're limiting me to *one?* [Laughs, then frowns.] The first that comes to mind isn't one I had much to do with. Grace Kelly. Now it's out in the light, what a skirt-lifting little phony she was, before she became a virgin bride and a princess.

BH: **I thought you might say your *Rebecca* costar, Joan Fontaine. Didn't you call her a phony, publicly?**

JA: Yes, I did, and yes, she is. We've had words, in public. I don't intend to give her any more publicity by continuing.

BH: **You've been described as having a Plantagenet profile....**

JA: I do, don't I? [Sighs.] Finally getting used to it. Old age softens our profiles.

BH: **You worked with the apparently heterosexual Hitchcock, and there are more gay undertones in his films, or say, Howard Hawks's, than in those of gay directors like Cukor and Arzner.**

JA: Do you mean because the Cukors and Arzners were repressing it in their work?

BH: **Yes, because being in the closet, they didn't want it to reflect on them. Most gay-themed films have been directed by nongay men—and virtually all the lesbian films, as well. But I mean, in the old days, gay undertones. As in *Rebecca*....**

JA: I wondered if we'd come to that. I know it's fashionable now to say that Mrs. Danvers in *Rebecca* was a spiteful lesbian. Spiteful, undoubtedly. But whoever in the picture called her a lesbian? Tell me that?

BH: **No one did—and that word wasn't allowed in films then. But the keys to her likely lesbianism are in the character herself and in her creator, Daphne Du Maurier, who biographers are disclosing was lesbian or bisexual.**

JA: Something to that effect did reach my ears. I've read and heard it argued that Olivier's role was secretly gay. I don't become aroused by it nor argue the theory. What do I care? I always assumed Olivier was gay. He was another phony....It's clear in the movie that he didn't love Rebecca, because she was beautiful and sensuous.

BH: **But Mrs. Danvers did. She's fanatically loyal to the deceased woman who called her Danny. She's still enchanted by her. And Du Maurier wrote her.**

JA: I know that an increasing number of Hitchcock films are coming under scrutiny. I know he had several secretly gay characters, and I believe he had his own inner struggles. But he doesn't seem to have been interested in lesbian characters, and I feel that Mrs. Danvers was spiteful and sexless. A frank sadist. She couldn't stand poor phony little Joan Fontaine, and I don't blame her. So much for *Rebecca*.

BH: Okay. Your stage characters have been as wicked. One might say you often played spinsters with a razor-sharp edge.

JA: Then you'd be wrong! Some of my characters were sexless—like Mrs. Danvers. [Defiantly.]...But many were married. I've played dreadful women from *Lady Scarface*—a murderous fiend—to *Medea* on the stage—she was married to Jason. I got raves as Lady Macbeth, a sadistic wife, but everyone forgets I was Big Mama in the film of *Cat On a Hot Tin Roof* [1958]. She was a long time married to Big Daddy [Burl Ives], and he was the bully in the family. I was just a devoted Southern wife with a handkerchief and a husband who couldn't stand her. [Giggles.] Tennessee Williams informed me that all his gentlemen friends were convinced it was a stretch for me to play a heterosexual!

BH: ...And was it?

JA: [Draws up proudly.] I am an actress. One of the leading actresses of my generation.

BH: Admittedly, it was one of your few sympathetic roles.

JA: I don't mind such a role once in a while, if it's in a good or a very popular film.

BH: What about your real-life marital record?

JA: Hah! I've had two husbands, but what does that really prove?

BH: That you took the plunge twice?

JA: Jumping into an ice-cold lake is also unpleasant, but the shock is over sooner....See here, I'm not unwilling to reveal that neither experience was a jolly holiday. But I already have. Why prolong the boredom? [Mock-yawns.]

BH: If it's painful [she nods], you don't need to discuss it.

JA: I know I don't!

BH: But in researching you, I found in a 1984 issue of the total-ly pro-marital *People* magazine that you described "my marriages" as "disastrous" and "ugly and despicable. They were very short, but too long."

JA: I'm not blaming myself. I didn't marry myself.

BH: The question arises, if the first was so awful, why try it a second time? [No reply.] Did hope spring eternal?

JA: You mean infernal?

BH: Did the second one being a theatrical producer make it more of a business partnership? Or a marriage of convenience?

JA: I don't have to explain myself to anyone.

BH: No. But with some women, especially when they're younger and less self-defined, marriage might be a way of explaining or justifying oneself to society.

JA: Hah! I was almost forty, the first time.

BH: I know, I have the years and dates. I meant generally.

JA: It's still a mess for a lot of individuals. I *am* an individ-ual, should have known better. We do things which when we're even older we cannot understand or explain, even to ourselves....I had an Aussie friend who said that prehistoric men believed that women thought love and reproduction were the same thing, and the result of those primitive men's mistaken stupidity was this mess called marriage.

BH: Doesn't it depend how one defines marriage? The legal definition is a straight-and-narrow one.

JA: You can define it, and you can keep it! I think it's one of men's more sustained failures. Mankind's. Anyway, men only care what other men think. For most men, women are to *have*, and other men are the reason men have wives. They'd be more content with girlfriends or whores.

BH: Well, most men are homosocial. They prefer the company and common interests, and, as you said, opinions of other men. Do you think women are as homosocial as men?

JA: I don't. I think most women value their male friends above their female ones.

BH: **That boils down to sexism and low self-esteem.**

JA: Probably. But at least women can have male friends. Usually platonic gay friends. Men don't have platonic female friends, they can only relate to women as sexual entities.

BH: **Dame Judith, you sound like a feminist!**

JA: I'm interested in my own self-interest. But I'm not going to argue sexual politics with anyone. I don't really care.

BH: **As you say, heterosexual men rarely see women as potential "just" friends. Gay men make friends with women of any sexuality. Why do you think average men don't befriend lesbians?**

JA: Someone asked me this, recently. I didn't think he meant it, thought it was just a rhetorical question. Why? Let's be honest, most lesbians are not sexually attracting to men.

BH: **Therefore why can't they be platonic friends?**

JA: I think men are threatened. Lesbians can be strong and all those masculine qualities that men so overrate. Men like to think only *they* can be, well, butch. When a girl is butch, I don't know, but maybe it threatens...or he thinks she's mocking him.

BH: **What about "lipstick lesbians," those who would be attractive to most men? They're not threatening. Why can't men make friends with them?**

JA: If she's a lesbian who can pass, then a man won't believe—refuses to believe, and I've known such situations—that she's not attracted to men. He may believe she likes other girls, but he won't believe she doesn't ...have *that* desire.

BH: **That she isn't magnetically drawn to his manhood, metaphorically or specifically speaking?**

JA: Don't get too specific, I'm not interested either. Most men are physically repulsive. Naked. But I take your point— it's baffling that straight women will often have gay men friends, but straight men don't have lesbian friends. I'm convinced it's one of the motives why lesbians lie to men—they don't want to be rejected. It's the men....

BH: **It's also the women. Why do they care if the people— men—they don't want to sleep with "reject" them?**

JA: I refuse to argue, but you cannot deny that in the world, and the movie world, too, it's the men who have the say- so, they have power, influence, and approval.

BH: **Those who seek others' approval are never free.**

JA: Who said that?

BH: **I don't know, but it stuck in my mind. Goethe said something pertinent: "The greatest evil that can befall a man is that he should come to think ill of himself." I think that's word for word. [It is.]**

JA: It applies to both sexes. [Nods.] But *why?* Why don't men want to have a friend of a gay woman?

BH: **I think men are more uncomfortable when traditional roles aren't strictly observed. Women are more comfortable with or tolerant of difference or ambiguity. After all, it's men that decided and enforce gender and sexual roles.**

JA: Most women do go along with it.

BH: **Patriarchal women.**

JA: The ones who call God "He."

BH: **Yes. They go along with what men decided.**

JA: I don't. I never did. Men want women to feel lonely without them. Everyone does. For years, people were on at me about giving too much time to my acting, and no time to a man.

BH: **What did you tell those overly concerned people?**

JA: It depended who they were. Some I ignored, others I told to go to Hades. Even after my feelings crystallized into words, I didn't bother explaining. But I feel most people aren't strong enough to be an *I*. They have to join another person, or group or church or organization, and be a *we*. I always wanted to be an *I*.

BH: **It's harder to be controlled by others if you're an *I*.**

JA: The older I get, the more immaterial other people's convictions and suggestions are for me.

BH: **You seem impervious to public opinion. Are you?**

JA: [Laughs.] I am now! But not to casting directors. I want to keep my hand in. To act when and if I wish to.

BH: **Your health seems excellent...?**

JA: I'm fine, if you don't ask for details. [Coughs.] You've not seen all my films [a declaration].

BH: **You didn't make enough of them. I've seen almost all your feature films, very few of your TV films.**

JA: Snob?

BH: **A moviegoer, mostly. Or an old movies buff on TV....The only other film [than *Cat*] I recall feeling sorry for you was *The Furies*. You were a conniver, but it's one of the most brutal things I've seen in film, when Stanwyck hurls the scissors into your face. The act, the weapon, and your reaction. Your acting.**

JA: You liked it.

BH: **No! But it was terribly effective. And when we finally saw you again in that movie, you got all the sympathy. The disfigurement had destroyed your spirit.**

JA: It also made her alcoholic....I miss period pictures...costumes, hairstyles. [Shrugs.]

BH: **You know what period role I can see you in? Lady Bracknell in Wilde's *The Importance of Being Earnest*.**

JA: I know the play. The trouble is, producers and casting people say I overwhelm most roles. "Too aggressive."

BH: **Or frightening? [She laughs.] But other than Dame Edith Evans—I had the pleasure of interviewing her—you're the only actress I can imagine as Bracknell.**

JA: Those shortsighted "experts" don't recall that I can play passive. I can act left, down, up, or right! [Clenches fist.]

BH: **They don't give you credit for being able to reign in some of your...overwhelmingness.**

JA: [Laughs.] That's what one calls it. [Frowns.] Who else have you had the pleasure [sarcastically] of interviewing?

BH: **Well, so many people. Um, Nancy Kulp—of "The Beverly Hillbillies." I always thought that in a less sexist time, she could have played the professor on "Gilligan's Island."**

JA: Odious program!...Is she the lesbian?

BH: **She's *a* lesbian. I suppose Sappho was *the* lesbian.**

JA: [No reaction.] When did you interview her?

BH: **Last year.**

JA: Was that island show in the 1960s? Why a professor?

BH: **I meant she could have played the role well. But at that time, a female character with brains couldn't also have power.**

JA: If she had power, she had to act stupid.

BH: **Or sexy. And if she was smart and capable, she was a secretary like Miss Hathaway, Nancy's role on "The Beverly Hillbillies."**

JA: Another odious show.

BH: **Snob?**

JA: Of course! [Smiles.] Was your Miss Kulp forthcoming about her...about herself? I've always heard she is gay.

BH: **She made it clear she is. She's very likable, very nice.**

JA: Likable! [Snorts.] Most people in this line of work who seem nice are putting up a well-practiced façade.

BH: **I think that's true of most *stars*. But Nancy Kulp is a fine person. I like her a lot. She reminded me of the older sister I never had.**

JA: How *sweet*....Miss Kulp is too old to be your sister. [Yawns.] At least she hasn't run to fat. But...most lesbians look more lesbian, the older they get. It comes out....I saw a recent photograph of her in a necktie, and she looked like an advertisement for lesbian liberation....

BH: **The older one gets, the more difficult it is to keep one's weight down. Such willpower is admirable.**

JA: [Glares.] I heard you interviewed Dorothy Arzner, the gay director you already named, with George Cukor.

BH: **How did you know that? It hasn't been published yet.**

JA: What are you waiting for? She's *dead*.

BH: **Yes, eleven years ago. But how did you know?**

JA: I know lots of things.

BH: **...Do you think old age confers greater wisdom?**

JA: No, I don't. There are more old fools than anyone could possibly count.

BH: **Did you know Ms. Arzner?**

JA: One of her former pupils worked for me. She said the first time she laid eyes on Miss Arzner, she thought she was a man.

BH: **She wore man-type clothes. But never pants—not in any photo I've seen. Other than riding pants.**

JA: She didn't dare! In that period, if she'd worn trousers in public, they might have stoned her. [Smiles.]

BH: **I guess only a beauteous type like Dietrich could get away with public pants?**

JA: Arzner had a well-known passion for Marlene, but Marlene rejected her. She preferred more feminine lesbians.

BH: **Yet some of Dietrich's female lovers were butch ones — Mercedes De Acosta, Nancy Spain, Jo Carstairs,...**

JA: I don't know about that. But as gay women grow older and become more masculine, they grow more used to non-feminine women — I would venture to say.

BH: **Dame Judith, would it bother you, being thought lesbian?**

JA: Many people already do....[Leering defiantly.]

BH: **May I ask your romantic orientation?**

JA: [Only slightly surprised, or hiding it well.] I am no romantic! *That* is my orientation!

BH: **You are for gay and lesbian equal rights?**

JA: I'm for everyone's rights, mostly my own. I do not associate myself with anyone — group or individual.

BH: **So when people think you're lesbian, does it bother you?**

JA: It doesn't bother me, it's they who bother me.

BH: **If you were gay, would you ever come out? [No reply; glares and clenches both fists. I know the interview is over, so ask:] If you came out now, at ninety-plus, how could it possibly harm you?**

JA: It couldn't! But I wouldn't "come out" in a million years. Why should I? I owe *nothing!* I don't owe anyone any explanations, and I won't join up with anything. Ever. They never gave *me* anything, and I certainly don't need them. I live my own life, and good luck to them, but leave me alone! Everybody, just leave me *alone!!*

AGNES MOOREHEAD

(1 9 0 6 – 1 9 7 4)

Leading ladies sometimes have golden faces or tresses and hearts of stone. Her friends said Agnes Moorehead had a face of stone and a heart of gold. Considered by many to be Hollywood's leading character actress, Moorehead told the press, "I suppose you could call me a character star."

The redhead's first two movies, Orson Welles's *Citizen Kane* and *The Magnificent Ambersons* (1941 and '42), feature on most cineastes' lists of the best American films. Moorehead segued from playing mothers to stereotyping as a well-coiffed bitch. Her sharp features and prickly personality led her to enact shrews, harridans, witches, nuns, sophisticates, pioneers, murderers, royalty, acting coaches, and at least one madam. She portrayed rich and poor but was in her element as women of means and brains who weren't afraid to throw it around or go it alone.

Ironically, the wide-ranging and notably unmaternal thespian became best known, at least to younger generations, for her eight-year stint on the small screen as Endora, the vinegary mother of Elizabeth Montgomery on "Bewitched." The 1964 to 1972 series about witches trying to pass for just plain folk boasted a number of gay and possibly gay performers: Darren II was Dick Sargent, who came out of the closet in 1991 on National Coming Out Day (as did another sitcom hetero-character, the man-crazy Zelda of "Dobie Gillis" fame, in real life lesbian lawyer Sheila James Kuehl). In 1992 Sargent served as co-Grand Marshal of the Los Angeles Gay Pride Day Parade with Montgomery.

Also in '92, one of the twins who played Tabitha—Darren and Samantha's witchlet daughter—declared herself a lesbian activist. And there was irrepressibly gay comedian Paul Lynde, aka Sam's Uncle Arthur; rumored-gay Shakespearean actor Maurice Evans, who played Sam's warlock father; and lifelong bachelor George Tobias, aka Mr. Kravitz.

Then there was Agnes Moorehead. In 1992 Ms. Montgomery told *The Advocate*, "I've heard rumors, but I never talked with her about them.

"I don't know if they were true. It was never anything she felt free enough to talk to me about. I wish that Agnes had felt she could trust me. It would have been nice. She was a very closed person in many ways. We were very fond of one another, but it never got personal."

Paul Lynde stated in *Out/Look* magazine, "The whole world knows Agnes was a lesbian—I mean, classy as hell, but one of the all-time Hollywood dykes....Agnes got a bit puritanical in her old age. She was known for giving great Hollywood parties, but she took against alcohol and smoking. More for health, I think. She wasn't one of those gay or bi

DRAMATIC ACTRESSES: *Agnes Moorehead* / 179

good-time Charlenes who later gets touched by religion and turns homophobic, like that wife of that cowboy actor."

Lynde was a platonic friend of actor-director Jerry Paris of "The Dick Van Dyke Show." Lynde appeared in Paris's film *How Sweet It Is!* (1968), starring Debbie Reynolds. "Filming *Sweet*, we were on a ship en route to Acapulco and our director [Paris] and much of the cast would sit around and dish. Jerry's worked with lesbians big and small, and he's a movie buff and poured forth everything he's heard or knew about Agnes and others, including some I don't dare identify.

"It seems Agnes was more easygoing when she first hit Hollywood. She had a succession of intimate lady friends she'd often go out with, and there were rumors, but it was all kept in the show biz family....When one of her husbands was caught cheating, so the story goes, Agnes screamed at him that if he could have a mistress, so could she!"

Another source on Moorehead's "firm preference for the ladies" was Elsa Lanchester, via Charles Laughton, who in the 1950s shared the stage with Agnes in Shaw's *Don Juan in Hell*. "Miss Moorehead was the soul of discretion. More than she needed to be—secondary actresses don't dwell in the same goldfish bowls reserved for stars....Someone who knew her extremely well says that Agnes is no longer 'active' that way, but she's always had romantic friendships with other women."

The waspish Lanchester recalled, "When television was in its infancy, I was in the running to play Madame Defarge [in *A Tale of Two Cities*]. It was a role I relished, but it went to Miss Moorehead. They tried to assure me it was nothing personal, Miss Moorehead was simply a bigger name. I ask you!"

John Houseman directed a national touring company of *Don Juan in Hell* that starred Myrna Loy as Doña Ana. While trying to cast the role, Houseman had announced, "I want a female in this role, a *real* woman." Some critics felt Moorehead had played Doña Ana "rather austerely."

Lee Van Cleef was in Howard Hughes's Mongol epic *The Conqueror* (1956). He wasn't the only one to note Moorehead's enduring crush on heterosexual friend and frequent costar Susan Hayward. "Agnes had it bad for Susan, but she could always mask it as sisterly or motherly affection, and Susan didn't seem to mind. They went way back." Though twelve years apart in age, the actresses would die within a year of each other from cancer contracted in southern Utah on location for *The Conqueror.*

Other actors in the film who died from radiation's effects included the pro-nuclear John Wayne, Van Cleef, and Pedro Armendariz—the Mexican star shot himself when he learned he had inoperable cancer.

A minister's daughter, Agnes Moorehead was born in Clinton, Massachusetts. At three she made her show biz bow on a radio show sponsored by her father, who moved the family to Wisconsin. She received a master's degree from the University of Wisconsin and in the 1930s became a stage actress, frequently essaying roles well older than herself.

During the Depression, acting jobs were scarce, and Agnes had to trade theater for radio, where her looks didn't limit her choice of roles. Her big break was being discovered by Orson Welles. She was a founding member of his Mercury Theater, and Welles called her the best-ever radio actress. Before Barbara Stanwyck starred in the 1948 film of *Sorry, Wrong Number*, Moorehead played it on radio, to raves. Later, there was friction between the two strong actresses.

On a 1970s Los Angeles radio talk show, the host tsk-tsked that Moorehead had never won an Oscar. She snapped, "Neither has Barbara Stanwyck!" Changing her tone to regretful amazement, she added, "Greta Garbo never won the

Academy Award either." Stanwyck's friend William Holden averred that the uniformly favorable reviews for Moorehead may have prejudiced Stanwyck's chance for an Oscar for *Sorry, Wrong Number* (it was her fourth and final A.A. nomination; Agnes was thrice nominated).

With her rather hatchet-like nose and chin, Moorehead moved from leading parts on radio to flashy support on screen, often stealing scenes with little effort from star leads. She participated in more than sixty films, spent seven years at MGM, and at fifteen hundred dollars a week was one of filmdom's top-paid supporters. Elsa Lanchester conceded, "She went as high as anyone could who was never first-billed." Elsa should have known; even for the title role of *The Bride of Frankenstein*, she wasn't first, second or third-billed. "Monstrous!" she huffed.

That Moorehead's private life was beyond the glare of the limelight had as much to do with press noninterest as her own reticence and ladylike demeanor. Twice married and twice divorced, she adopted a son named Sean who according to the Academy's library in Beverly Hills "was believed to have vanished several years before she died" of lung cancer at sixty-seven.

In 1972 I was writing for the college newspaper in Santa Barbara. I knew that Agnes Moorehead often came up the coast to lecture to women's groups or visit friends. She'd recently completed her tenure as Endora and was quoted in the local paper as hoping to spend more time in S.B. I thought a non-Endora interview would be a plum for my paper and soon obtained Moorehead's home address in Beverly Hills.

She lived on North Roxbury Drive, several mansions opposite Lucille Ball, her leading lady in the 1942 classic *The Big Street*. Moorehead's secretary sent back a monogrammed note saying that A.M. was flattered by the request but had no more room in her '72 schedule, though please try again.

I did, in '73, by which time I'd read up on her and been told by those who knew or worked with her that she was gay, lesbian, asexual, bisexual, frigid where men were concerned, a prudish bull-dyke, a closet femme, or a latent heterosexual. My second request yielded a telephone number. I called, and the date was set at Villa Agnese (pronounced Ahn-yay-zay), Ms. Moorehead's Italianate home with its painted archway, previously owned by composer Sigmund Romberg.

In the late 1980s, by which time I was living in Beverly Hills, the villa's latest owners remodeled—and painted over!—what was one of the little town's most recognizable and distinguished residences. Unlike the unique and imposing actress, the house's features and character were finally altered and standardized.

BH: My mother's favorite star—and she resembles her—is Susan Hayward, one of your most memorable costars.

AM: Susan is one of the best.

BH: And a rare mixture of beauty and toughness. I remember you both in *Untamed* and an earlier, ethereal picture set in Venice where she wore a beautiful gown and looked stunning.

AM: Yes, and I was an old, old crone. It was *The Lost Moment* [1947], a class of movie they don't make anymore, with romance and beauty, culture—wonderful music, piano—and fantasy. What is wrong with fantasy?

BH: Nothing. There should be room for fantasy and realism. With so much realism, sometimes one welcomes the really old movies.

AM: I think anything in black and white has a fantasy quality.

BH: Even film noir. Speaking of realism, it was a jolt to see you as Velma, the maid to Bette Davis in *Hush...Hush, Sweet Charlotte* [1964]. You even wore rags, and your hair was ratty.

AM: [Laughing.] My dear boy! I hope you didn't think I'd come down in the world! I had a wonderful time doing it.

BH: Wasn't Joan Crawford supposed to costar in it?

AM: [Producer-director] Robert Aldrich wanted it to be a sequel [to *What Ever Happened to Baby Jane?*], but Bette had them change the title, and I believe some of the script. She also made it possible for Miss Crawford to exit the film, then replaced her with her friend Olivia De Havilland.

BH: Ah. I met an author at a cocktail party who said that the screen's two greatest character actresses were you and Thelma Ritter. Did you two get along?

AM: [Startled.] I'm certain we must have. Why?

BH: He said you never competed for the same roles because you specialized in ladies and she in dames, as he called them.

AM: [Amused.] That is so, with exceptions. As you saw, I could and did play a maid, and Miss Ritter was versatile enough to play a...a Mrs. Rittenhouse type.

BH: Margaret Dumont's role. Do you know anything about the private life of Ms. Dumont?

AM: No. Why do you ask?

BH: Because we often learn more than we care to about stars but next to nothing about more interesting supporting players. All I've heard is that Dumont had one husband, no kids, and was bald as a cueball. None of which really says what the woman was like.

AM: So you find when you like an actress, you want to know more about her?

BH: Definitely. The same with authors. After several books, or films, one wants to know more about the source of that pleasure.

AM: You're not afraid of finding out something disappointing?

BH: It can happen. I know people who can't stomach a Ronald Reagan movie, but I know that while I'm appalled by Vanessa Redgrave's anti-Israel cant, her talent is often fascinating to watch.

AM: I would not care to be one of these younger actresses now. We worked on our work. They work on their image—their public life and publicity. What has that got to do with acting?

BH: It just has to do with being a celebrity.

AM: It's a lack of class. If an actress cannot become a personality through her work, she cannot, or should not, become one through her comings and goings.

BH: Either one has personality or one doesn't?

AM: Yes. It shows up in the performances. It does not accrue from dating or marrying and divorcing famous actors.

BH: Elizabeth Taylor is one star who is famous for her work and her personal life.

AM: A good actress, but I would say more famous, or a bigger star at the box office, for her private life.

BH: For her men....

AM: I would never care to have my work compete with my latest relationship, connubial or otherwise.

BH: Does it seem odd not to be doing "Bewitched" anymore?

AM: It was a lengthy stretch. In a way, it's a relief to be done. I hope to move on to other things.

BH: Do you think Endora stereotyped you at all?

AM: No. How many witches can I play? What's a shame is that fewer movies are made now. Far fewer. This results in less work. I was prepared to work less at my age, but not...not this much less.

BH: **Most of your recent work is on TV, including telefilms.**

AM: You're going to ask about television versus film. I do know that most of my good work is behind me. But I am an actress, and to act, I have to accept the best of what is offered. I do prefer and miss motion pictures, but there's very little room in them for older people now.

BH: **Which seems odd when the average American is older now.**

AM: The "graying" of our population [sarcastically]. One wouldn't know it from what gets made these days!

BH: **Lately you've done some horror films like *What's the Matter with Helen?* [with Debbie Reynolds] and *Dear Dead Delilah*. [She grimaces at the titles' mention.] Would you have done such movies in the old days?**

AM: [Bristling.] I did a film called *The Bat* long ago [1959], with Vincent Price. Unlike Mr. Price, I did not immerse myself in that genre, but it was a respectable movie, from a popular play....In the one with Debbie, I was a guest star, as a lady preacher based on Aimee Semple McPherson. None of my scenes was bloody. Nor in the film with Bette Davis; I don't know what's in every movie I make because I don't watch them all. These days, one can get a nasty shock watching some of them....But I do avoid playing the same parts to where the public thinks of me as nothing else. It's very sad that stars like Miss Davis and Miss Crawford can do little other than chillers.

BH: **Somebody told me she felt your character of Kim Novak's coach and mentor in *Jeanne Eagels* [1957] was lesbian.**

AM: [Eyebrows higher, lids lower.] It was not written that way. She was a composite character, and Jeanne Eagels was a real person.

BH: Yes, but you know that non-heterosexual characters, based on real people or not, weren't permitted on screen from 1934 to circa 1959. However, the coach was fiercely protective of and did seem to be in love with Eagels.

AM: With two women, it's more difficult to know where love leaves off and the other begins. With men, it's clearer.

BH: You mean love and yearning. But love often includes yearning, and yearning sometimes includes love. Your character had no man in her life; her life revolved around Jeanne.

AM: Well, have it your way.

BH: Not my way, but realistically. It isn't necessarily so, but it's probable. I know there have been lesbian acting coaches; one famous one was Minna Wallis, Hal's sister.

AM: [Smiles.] You're well informed, my boy. But she became a famous agent. Few are content merely to coach; it's very humbling.

BH: Really? I think the difference between your characters is that the maid [in *Charlotte*] is loyal to Davis, while the coach is loving to Novak.

AM: Kim is more comely than Miss Davis, but at any rate I played the parts as written. The scenarist would have to tell you if either character was conceived as being in love with another woman.

BH: Did it ever bother you being labeled "vinegary," "acerbic," or the other adjectives which reviewers and interviewers use?

AM: My colleagues sometimes tell me things they read. My friends know that most of the time I prefer not to bother.

BH: A friend of mine who's a musician said she saw you in the 1950s on TV—"Camera Three"?—reading from the diaries of the harpsichordist Wanda Landowska.

AM: [Remembering...suddenly delighted.] Did she?! And she remembers? That's very nice! It was "Camera Three." Yes, television had much more class...it was even blatantly cultural.

BH: If not realistic. Did you know that the great Landowska was lesbian?

AM: Was she really? [Surprised.] She was married....

BH: Pardon me, but that means nothing.

AM: "Nothing"?! Marriage is a....

BH: I meant that most famous lesbians have been married at some time....

AM: I see. Well, thank you for informing me. I suppose you read this in a book?

BH: Yes, a Landowska biography. A complete one—not the sort that omits what it disapproves of. Before I forget, what was the original title of *Hush...Hush, Sweet Charlotte*?

AM: Let's see...*What Ever Became of Cousin Charlotte?*

BH: Did I hear correctly that you sing?

AM: I have always used my voice. I can sing—most people don't know that. I do readings, recordings, I teach acting....

BH: You should teach acting. You were much more believable [in *Dragon Seed*, 1944] as a Chinese than Katharine Hepburn.

AM: Why, thank you.

BH: As you said, you used your voice. You sounded like what Chinese are supposed to sound like in movies. Ms. Hepburn sounded Bryn Mawr all the way. [She smiles widely.] Do you agree that most supporting actors have more talent than stars?

AM: There are exceptions, but most stars are hired for their looks, and we despite ours. We have a better chance to grow, in more variegated roles.

BH: **Star actresses basically play themselves, or not?**

AM: Many of them earn more but act less. [With a fixed smile.]

BH: **What do you think of men writing most women's roles?**

AM: I think we need more ladies at the typewriters. [Grins.]

BH: **Three of your first four films were via Orson Welles. Do you think if it hadn't been for him, you might not have worked much on screen until you turned forty?**

AM: But you see, I began in movies in my mid-thirties. Very late.

BH: **Would you have been offered many screen roles in your twenties?**

AM: Not as many as I later was. There's the actress who works mostly before forty and the one who works mostly after forty.

BH: **You costarred in two movies which teamed Jane Wyman and Rock Hudson as lovers. Did you know he was gay? [Nods.] How?**

AM: An informant. Our profession is full of wanted and unwanted informants....He's a good actor. Whatever you think of his and Jane's chemistry, the first film, *Magnificent Obsession* [1954] made him into a matinee idol. A "sex symbol" for the ladies.

BH: **For the interested public. Do you think a gay or lesbian star has more enemies than a heterosexual star?**

AM: I've certainly never been asked that question before! [Grins.] On the question of enemies, it's difficult. Everyone says he or she is your friend. No one is willing to admit to malice.

BH: **Even in an industry so full of it?**

AM: Especially!

BH: **You almost played lesbian in *The Revolt of Mamie Stover* [1956]. As the madam to Jane Russell.**

AM: I would have but for censorship. They got cold feet. It could have been done five years later.

BH: **But in the Eisenhower era, no? Your character was not only stripped of her lesbianism, but her profession. In the finished movie, it's not even clear that you're a madam.**

AM: It's clear to some people....Hollywood likes to profit from sensational topics without being sensational.

BH: **Other than the madam's dialogue, how if at all would you have conveyed that the woman was lesbian?**

AM: I wouldn't have resorted to anything old-fashioned—I'd wear high-heels, regardless. I might have injected an extra dose of severity into her dealings with men and a little more tenderness when she was with Mamie or her young favorites.

BH: **In 1961 Barbara Stanwyck did play a clearly lesbian madam. What did you think of her performance in *Walk On the Wild Side*?**

AM: I...never saw it.

BH: **Did you ever hear rumors about Ms. Stanwyck? [Blank reaction.] You know, from an informant? Like about Rock Hudson?**

AM: [Shocked or alarmed.] We're not here to talk about... other stars.

BH: **You were in what has become a lesbian cult classic, *Caged* [1950]. *The* women's prison movie.**

AM: An *important* movie because it helped ameliorate conditions throughout the penal system, I was assured.

BH: **That's right. It was also one of the first movies to bring up lesbianism, although in an unsavory context and even though each sapphic character had to express interest in men.**

AM: As I said, Hollywood likes to have it both ways. [Smiling.] *My* character was the film's conscience—she had nothing to do with sex, one way or the other.

BH: Hope Emerson, as the huge matron, is a standout in *Caged*.

AM: She certainly was.

BH: Did you play Debbie Reynolds's mother in *How the West Was Won*? [No reply.] I remember you did a voice in [the animated] *Charlotte's Web*, which also had Debbie Reynolds. [No reaction.]...Ms. Reynolds and Susan Hayward are probably your most frequent leading ladies, aren't they?

AM: [Teeth somewhat clenched.] I don't want to discuss actors.

BH: May one inquire as to what your husbands did for a living? [Silence.] Or why you divorced?

AM: A divorce is a regrettable action, not a fit conversational topic. Nor has it anything to do with Hollywood.

BH: Marriages often do have to do with Hollywood. But divorces often correct a mistake.

AM: A mistake that big may take more than a divorce to set it right.

BH: Were your marriages happy?

AM: If they were, I'd still be in them.

BH: Do you think actresses should marry?

AM: Only if they want children.

BH: I understand you have a son?

AM: I don't discuss any of my family.

BH: What do you think of Hollywood lesbians?

AM: Which ones?

BH: So there *are* lesbians in Hollywood?

AM: [Smiles.] Of course there are. Everywhere. Most of them are nice people and not promiscuous—like the men.

BH: Gay men?

AM: All men.

BH: What do you think of the word "lesbian"?

AM: [Shrugs.] I think "sapphic" is an improvement, but I don't care for "homosexual" at all. Women are not homosexual. It's a very masculine word.

BH: How can a lesbian not be homosexual? Unless she's bi-sexual?

AM: I don't like the comparing....I mean, not that it matters to me. Men are this-sexual or that-sexual, but females, in that sense, are a different species. A woman may love a person who is this or that, male or female. *Love* doesn't have a sex. It's men who always have to bring sex— and...activities—into everything. They can't help being heterosexual, homosexual or the other one. Women operate on a different plane; the feelings are emotional, not physical.

BH: So you're pleased that homosexual men are called "gay," and...women are lesbians or...

AM: Or not lesbians, it doesn't matter so much with females. It's not the same difference as with men.

BH: There's no lust? [She shrugs.] Have you always thought this?

AM: One comes around to certain conclusions or hopes.

BH: So in other words, a woman can have lesbian feelings but not be homosexual?

AM: I think so. Why bring up "sex"? That's men's concern. Or habit. *They* talk that way and want to drag women down to their level, to have no class. Young women are often *very* willing.

BH: Have you loved many women?

AM: Well, I have loved women. Of course.

BH: More than your husbands?

AM: That's rather rude. But love and marriage don't always go together. Despite the song.

BH: So marriage is often a duty thing?

AM: Of course it is. But now I think you should...

BH: Just one more question. Numerous Hollywood actresses—Garbo, Gish, Dietrich, Jean Arthur, um, Kay Francis, Stanwyck, Bankhead, Del Rio, Janet Gaynor, etc., etc.— have enjoyed lesbian or bi relationships. Have you ever...?

AM: Yes, you'd love to put me in their excellent company! Even if I don't belong in the same category. [Smiles wryly.]

BH: You don't?

AM: Those ladies were more beautiful than me.

BH: Off the record? I can turn off the tape recorder.

AM: Leave it on, leave it on. [Sighs.] You apparently have your own informants [half smiles]. I don't know what you've heard, and I don't want to hear, and some of it may even be true.

BH: The truth gets around.

AM: ...Somehow.

BH: Would the truth hurt you professionally, now?

AM: Now? Probably not. But I don't want anyone misinterpreting what was beautiful and even spiritual. I haven't penned my memoirs and doubt that there will be—I *hope* there won't be—a book purporting to represent my life. My work, anyone can see. I never really cared to share anything with the public, or very many people, besides my work.

BH: As a supporting actress, you'll be a part of many books and biographies of major Hollywood stars.

AM: That was rude, too.

BH: **I meant that having been in so many famous movies, with so many legendary stars, your name and face—in movie stills—will be in so many books yet to come.**

AM: You've just presented my case, in a way. Let's suppose a biography is written of...Jean Arthur. She had her life, her work, a husband or two, no children, and different people thought different things about her. She was emotionally intricate. Most women are. Actresses, more so. An entire book could put much of Jean Arthur, and what she did and who she loved, into perspective. It would take an entire book, at least.

No such book is forthcoming for me. If I make a statement to you now, it will be used and misinterpreted, and one way or another will represent me, if it's controversial or shocking enough, in who knows how many future books? On the screen or in a book, even a famous supporting actress never receives the same in-depth... the amount of time that any star, great or indifferent, always receives.

As an actress, I'm used to this. I have no option. As a person, I do. My life has been as long as any, I've had to struggle more than most people in my very privileged profession, and although my career might be described or capsulized in a few paragraphs by some writers, I won't let that happen to my life. Certainly not to my own private life...having others try to understand or illuminate me, all in the space of one or two pages or less—in a book about someone else! [Eyes have moistened.]

BH: **[Gently.] The solution is to write or collaborate on your own book.**

AM: It's one solution. The other is to do nothing, and inertia is the result of most of our struggles, my boy.

BH: **Your golden-age-of-Hollywood career deserves its own book.**

AM: I think it deserves it, too! And if I ever seriously consider doing my memoirs, I'll be in touch with you. You'll be older then. [Pause and a grin.] *I* won't be.

BH: **Don't you think as one gets older, there's more time to reflect on oneself and devote to one's memoirs?**

AM: More time, but less energy. Life tires one out—not a lot, but increasingly. One can't underestimate inertia.

BH: **Do you think fear of death inhibits some actors from writing an autobiography? The idea that if one's putting one's life on paper, most of it must be over?**

AM: Most of it *is* over. If someone writes his memoirs, he can't be that far from the end. For some, it's a fear of death. But I think for most people, there's more fear of life.

BH: **Fear of the truth of one's life?**

AM: And of exploring it fully or feeling everything one would like to. It's an unavoidable truth: fear of life closes off more opportunities for us than fear of death ever does.

BARBARA STANWYCK

(1 9 0 7 – 1 9 9 0)

The following of her film titles indicate something about Barbara Stanwyck: *The Locked Door, Illicit, Forbidden, Ladies They Talk About, Gambling Lady, The Secret Bride, The Bride Walks Out, This Is My Affair, Always Goodbye, Remember the Night, The Gay Sisters, Flesh and Fantasy, The Bride Wore Boots, The Strange Love of Martha Ivers, Variety Girl, The Other Love, The Lady Gambles, The File on Thelma Jordon, No Man of Her Own, The Furies, To Please a Lady, Clash By Night, Jeopardy, All I Desire, The Moonlighter, Blowing Wild, Cattle Queen of Montana, There's Always Tomorrow, The Maverick Queen, These Wilder Years,* and *Walk On the Wild Side.*

The above list doesn't include many of Stanwyck's more popular pictures, among them *Stella Dallas, The Mad Miss Manton, Ball of Fire, Golden Boy, The Lady Eve, Meet John Doe, Double Indemnity, Sorry, Wrong Number,* etc. But the first list is more telling.

Brooklynite Ruby Stevens became known as "Missy" to friends and film crews and as Barbara Stanwyck to generations of movie and then TV viewers. She was a screen star who debuted in 1927 and developed into a strong personality far more distinctive after age thirty than before. But she wasn't a true superstar, a real beauty, or widely considered a standout talent—four Oscar nominations, and she lost them all, eventually earning an honorary one. When the American Film Institute chose to honor her with its Life Achievement Award, she confessed she thought they'd made a mistake and had wanted Barbra Streisand.

Patsy Kelly, who worked for Stanwyck's first husband Frank Fay, felt "Barbara came up the hard way. She had a lot of hard knocks. She talks a tough game, but she has a lot of loneliness in her and she isn't so cocksure like she always pretends. But it was a very hard shell she built."

The hard knocks began early. Ruby was two when her mother was accidentally killed by being pushed off a moving trolley by a drunk and hitting her head on the pavement. Ruby's father, left to look after the three younger of his five offspring alone, soon abandoned his family to work in Panama. Elder sister Mildred was a show girl, often away on tour—Ruby would follow in her footsteps—and so the little girl and her elder brother were farmed out to one foster home after another.

At eleven she was placed with a Jewish couple, the Cohens. Decades later she declared, "They were the first people ever to brush my hair, care how I looked. They taught me how to use my knife and fork. They tried to teach me nice manners. They tried to stop me from swearing." However, at thirteen, Ruby quit school to go to work in a department store.

Show biz paid better. "She told me after we got to know each other," explained stage and screen costar Marjorie Main, "that being a chorus girl could be humiliating and dangerous. The rich men who didn't want to tangle with prostitutes would often hire show girls instead." As ex-show-girl Joan Crawford revealed, several high kickers were bi or lesbian, and in time each girl got propositioned by both genders.

At nineteen Ruby became a Broadway star. Also in 1926, two theater bigwigs reportedly renamed her after a thirty-year-old show: Jane Stanwyck in *Barbara Frietchie*. In 1927 she did her one silent movie, *Broadway Nights*. In 1928 she wed the much-older comic star Frank Fay. Hours later, she was on a train heading for a touring engagement. *Titanic* (1953) costar Clifton Webb said, "Two things Barbara doesn't address are her childhood and her first marriage."

Stanwyck advised *Photoplay*, "Whoever said childhood's the best time of your life was way off base. Mine's where it belongs, behind me. But people will go find out about it, and print things, and rake it over. If I'd been born earlier or in another country, they probably couldn't do that" (as with Judith Anderson). As for the marriage, it was rumored to be financially motivated on Barbara's part, though she kept on working. Fay had already had two wives and was heavily alcoholic, perhaps by this time impotent or inactive.

He was also, insiders stated, a wife beater. At the end of 1932, the two adopted a boy, Dion, apparently to save the marriage, which ended a few years later. The boy later left his mother against her wishes to join his touring father, eventually joining the army against her wishes and legally changing his first name. The last straw came when he sold his story to the press, publicly wondering why his adoptive mother didn't speak to him. She never did, after that.

Ironically, when Fay died in 1961, he didn't include Dion—by then Anthony—in his will. Anthony sued and won. Nor did Stanwyck ever see her grandchild, Anthony's son.

Meanwhile, she'd become a movie star, working frequently from early talkies on. She entered her golden age in 1937 with the popular *Stella Dallas*, acting steadily until 1957, when at fifty she left the big screen, later making a comeback in the pioneering lesbian role in *Walk On the Wild Side*. She did a few other sixties films before turning permanently to television, most notably in her western series "The Big Valley."

In 1939, via studio pressure, Stanwyck had wed costar and "too beautiful" actor Robert Taylor (née Spangler Arlington Brugh). According to many, including George Cukor, who directed Taylor in his breakthrough role in *Camille* (1936), Taylor was gay or bisexual. MGM's Louis B. Mayer (aka Louis B. Merde) felt Taylor wasn't manly enough and couldn't proceed toward full-fledged stardom until he ceased being pretty and single. So Taylor acquired a bride, a mustache, and he aged. He also grew increasingly conservative, and if gay, became bisexual via a second, younger wife (younger than him; he was four years' Stanwyck's junior) and offspring. During the 1950s, he took part in the McCarthy witchhunts, and after their marriage said he still respected and admired Barbara; they costarred in her last movie, the 1965 thriller *The Night Walker*.

Director Mitchell Leisen noted, "Barbara loved Bob, and it may have led to the bedroom....She wanted companionship, and as a star, she realized there were off-screen rules one lived by....They were an outdoorsy pair, best friends. It slayed her when he left her for that German actress" (Ursula Thiess).

Costar Ricardo Cortez (née Jacob Krantz) told *Liberty* magazine, "She's the toughest dame I ever worked with. She thinks like a man, but fortunately she doesn't look like no man!" Barbara's rumored lovers included Marlene Dietrich and close friend Joan Crawford. A nonadmirer was Bette Davis, who fought for the role won by Stanwyck (an Emmy, too) in "The Thorn Birds." *New York* magazine wrote that Stanwyck "acts as butchly matriarchal as she did when she roamed the sound stages of 'The Big Valley.'" Davis was quoted by her telltale daughter after they watched the hit miniseries on TV:

"Yagh! [Richard Chamberlain's] not even vaguely believable. He's totally sexless. And Stanwyck! God! She was awful! She wasn't the least bit sexy. Mary Carson was supposed to be a sexy broad....*I* should have played her."

In the 1950s and sixties Stanwyck found her niche on the big and small screens in westerns. She announced, "I'm mad about westerns, and no matter what anyone else tells you, this is all I want to do....I want to play a real frontier woman, not one of those crinoline-covered things you see in most westerns. I'm with the boys — I want to go where the boys go."

Her two most famous pet peeves were performers who weren't on time and actresses who fussed about their hair and makeup. "If people can't be on time — on the dot! — I don't want them around," she said of young actors.

Thus, when our two o'clock appointment at her home on Loma Vista Drive in Beverly Hills in 1987 was moved to 2:15, I feared being late. Or early. On the phone she'd explained rather warmly that she was more nonchalant about inviting strangers to the house since 1981, when a burglar had broken in, conked her on the head, locked her in the closet (no comment), and departed with jewels worth five thousand dollars. And she asserted, "Let's forego questions about my films and roles. *Walk On the Wild Side*, too...."

"The Thorn Birds" was only four years past, but the firm telephone voice belied the frail form and the careworn face I saw before me in her sunny, flowery home. The interview happened because of her friendship with a young then-star and award presenter whom I knew and who'd dialed Stanwyck in my presence, "introduced" me, then urged her to meet with me after I sent her my book "to like really prove he's a real writer."

BH: Thank you for inviting me to your charming home.

BS: I'm getting familiar with it in my old age.

BH: It must have been terrifying to not only be burglarized but manhandled?

BS: It was...the worst. You don't know what someone's going to do. He could have killed me.

BH: May I ask if a famous story is true? They say Loretta Young had a swear box on the set, and every time someone swore, she made him pay a nickel or a quarter. That one day you were on the set, and you uttered some word, and she pointed to the box, so you stuffed in a one-dollar or five-dollar bill and said something like, "Here, Loretta. Now I can say, 'Go f--- yourself.'" Is that true?

BS: [Smiling patiently.] No.

BH: What causes something like that to be repeated so often?

BS: She did have a swear box, but I never told her where to go—that's the other version of what I'm supposed to have said. I did cuss once in a while, but never at Loretta Young. [Beat.] She might have excommunicated me.

BH: She's been nicknamed Attila the Nun.

BS: We all have nicknames. Now, about your book...the Cukor interview I liked. The directors—I learned a lot. Even things I didn't need to know, about the drug-addict [Rainer Werner Fassbinder]. People should read that, it shows what drugs do to people insane enough to take them.

BH: One of your more notable quotes of late was when John Belushi died from a drug overdose. You said something like, Why should I feel sorry for him?—he's the one who chose drugs.

BS: What I said is on record. I stand by it. [Pained expression.] I'm annoyed by your Rock Hudson interview. It reveals so much, and you wrote in the preface that he wouldn't have wanted some of his comments made public. So why did you do it? Money?

BH: Truth. There's more money in selective-truth articles than nonfiction books. Everything Rock told me, he knew it was for eventual publication—part of the interviews did appear before his death. What I meant was that of the six men in the book, he was the biggest star, ergo the most closeted.

BS: He wasn't very closeted.

BH: He certainly was, publicly. A few years before his death, a British paper asked him the Big Question, and Rock denied it again.

BS: [Shaking head.] You have to understand that being the biggest star, he had the most to lose.

BH: And the most responsibility as a public figure and role model. By then he was past his professional prime, and from Duluth to Hong Kong, much of the public knew his reality. Yet if he'd lived, he wouldn't have come out....

BS: Why should he have to come out?

BH: For himself and for those like him. Why should it be pretended that no one famous or admired is gay or lesbian? How old or rich does a star have to be before they stop being selfish or scared?

BS: What was that you wrote about stars...and leashes?

BH: I said that of the sextet [Sal Mineo, George Cukor, Luchino Visconti, Cecil Beaton, Rainer Werner Fassbinder, and Hudson], Hudson was the most closeted because the greater the fame, the tighter the leash of public affection.

BS: That's it. That says it....I'm glad Hudson wasn't around to read how frank you were.

BH: How frank *he* was. He didn't answer every question, and he was pleased and relieved to finally be asked a lot of those questions.

BS: Questions that aren't asked of stars.

BH: Exactly. Or of anyone in public life. The difference between some of us and bigots is that we accept and celebrate who Rock really was, or Dorothy Arzner, while the bigots make them hide who they are and live in fear and denial.

BS: Well, men like to get things off their chests more.

BH: Yes, I've noticed women are more reticent about their private selves.

BS: Because there's more that can be used against them...fewer chances for a woman to make something of herself, and more chances to say the wrong thing and be criticized. Not in my case, but it hasn't gotten so much better with all the hollering and demonstrating for equal rights.

BH: Without that, nothing would change. No dominant group gives an oppressed group their rights without a struggle. [She shrugs.] But I agree with you. It's why actresses say less. If an actor says he's had ten girlfriends, fine; if an actress says she's had ten boyfriends, she can be stigmatized.

BS: She would be now. Before, she wouldn't—they'd keep it quiet. Or she'd keep her mouth shut. Now they make a big deal out of everything, so we can't tell them anything.

BH: Yes, but there's a difference between, say, promiscuous and therefore chosen behavior—like saying one's slept with several costars—and revealing an inherent fact about oneself, like Sal Mineo saying that he was gay.

BS: I didn't read it. But he was younger, he was able to say it with fewer repercussions. [Note: Mineo discussed Robert Taylor.]

BH: But this is one area where men are more discriminated against. If an actress or singer says she's bi, there's little fallout. If any actor does, he can lose a lot....

BS: If he's a star and the women out there are crazy about him.

BH: Yes, a sex symbol. By contrast, most comics or supporting performers have little or nothing to lose.

BS: It's better than it was for them. [Grudgingly.]

BH: Other than that, what would you say is the biggest disadvantage of being a female star?

BS: You recognize there are disadvantages...most writers and the fans think it's a bed of roses.

BH: Someone once said—probably a woman—"Life is a bed of roses, except for the pricks."

BS: [Laughs huskily.] Funny! There are times....One disadvantage is having a cold or a blemish. That minor fact may mean an actress can't do a close-up for days or a week.

BH: Hollywood is as sexist as ever in terms of looks, isn't it?

BS: It isn't. An actress still has to look special, but the picture-perfect standards of the past are...gone.

BH: And an extremely good-looking actor isn't penalized for it the way a Tyrone Power or Robert Taylor was, right?

BS: [Visibly stiffening.] In general.

BH: As with actresses, there's the notion that if a guy looks like a Ty Power or a Robert Redford, he can't be much of a talent.

BS: There are stars, there are actors, there are talented stars....

BH: Do you agree that Hollywood is a personality business?

BS: A looks and personality business.

BH: Can I bring up something controversial?

BS: You can if you're able. You *may*. [Smiles.] A leftover from school days. I knew you'd bring up something unpleasant.

BH: Controversy isn't always unpleasant. It's just what's disapproved of by most or by a vocal few. This is political, not sexual.

BS: ...Worse. Makes more enemies.

BH: And it's not directly about you.

BS: Then let's have it!

BH: Both your ex-husbands denounced people during the 1950s witchhunts.

BS: [Agitated.] They denounced communism!

BH: That's the concept. What they denounced were individuals suspected of being Communist Party members—when it wasn't illegal to belong—and people who were liberal, most of them Jewish or gay or sometimes both. It was a backlash, and Frank Fay denounced suspected "anti-Catholic communists." Many of them performers he'd known who went on to success while he became an alcoholic has-been.

BS: [Containing her rage.] Are you communist?

BH: That's the tactic....I am pro-*liberty*. Communism, like fascism, is dictatorial and extremely homophobic and anti-Semitic.

BS: You want to know whether I agreed with them?

BH: A husband or ex doesn't always represent his wife, but it was rare that an actress had two men in her life taking such active roles in that national, that human, tragedy.

BS: [Nostrils flaring.] Coincidence....I'm not about to rehash national history or Hollywood politics or put forth what I believe. If there's one more political question, or comment, we'll stop this conversation [acidly] of ours.

BH: No more politics. Believe me, I'm not pro-communist. It always works out badly, on so many levels.

BS: Well, I like hearing that.

BH: But right-wing religious fanatics are just as horrible. What women do you admire most?

BS: Why women?

BH: Because I'm asking one. An actress herself much-admired.

BS: [Inclines head.] I thank you for that, but as a public figure, I can't answer your question.

BH: Oh. Were you ever treated like window dressing, and if so, did you like it?

BS: [Chuckles.] There isn't a leading actress who hasn't been asked her measurements by reporters.

BH: When Melina Mercouri was asked that, she replied that actresses aren't cattle, that in Greece they measure an actress by her eyes, her soul, and her acting.

BS: [Drily.] Good answer.

BH: How did you answer the measurements question?

BS: It was so long ago, I'm not positive whether I answered him.

BH: A general question — what was your happiest time?

BS: Too broad. Stick to more specific ones. Like you normally do. One thing I also don't like about interviews I see in periodicals is the questions. It's why I don't read most of them. They ask his favorite color, food, or song...who *cares?* Or something so general, like his happiest moments.

Happiness is so personal. It's uncommon, and you *feel* it, you can't always put it into the proper words. It's not easy to share, and you can't make a snappy phrase or quote out of it.

BH: Unlike...grief?

BS: Unlike grief! Everyone wants to share their grief and talk about it. Not me! Why don't people share their happiness?

BH: **As you said, it's harder to describe. And if it has to do with love or sex or pride, it's very personal. Grief is more...universal.**

BS: Yes, we can all agree on tragedy, not on comedy.

BH: **That's true. We may laugh at different things, but who doesn't cry when a character loses a loved one?**

BS: Now we're getting somewhere. Or are you out of controversy?

BH: **Since you mention it....There's a list—*I* did not compile it—that came out in 1981 in a paper called the *Hollywood Star*, of seventy bisexual Hollywood actresses.**

BS: [Slowly.] I never saw it....

BH: **If you wanted to see it, I have the half page with the headline, and the full page, from inside, with the list of seventy.**

BS: You may show it to me. [I do, she unfolds the headline, then the full page list; the name on the top left is *Barbara Stanwyck*, but I don't dare congratulate her on her top billing. She studies the list, eyes opening wider a few times, then hands it back to me impassively.]

BH: **This followed a list they'd published of bisexual actors. Did you see on the top right? It says, "Although many of the listed actresses prefer both men and women, it has no bearing on their talent as actresses."**

BS: [Pause.] It's a star-studded list, isn't it?

BH: **Not in alphabetical order....**

BS: [Sharply.] I'd like you to give me the list. You don't mind [reaches for it; I yield it up].

BH: **I can loan it to you. I have no copy.**

BS: [After rereading the list.] What do *you* think of it?

BH: **Half of it is no surprise, a few names are very surprising. Like Susan Hayward. But of course it could mean just one such fling, in some instances. I don't think anyone would think any less of any of these actresses.**

BS: I don't believe all of it.

BH: **No one else ever knows all about a person's private life or encounters. I'm surprised at some of the actresses listed, because presumably they're not bi, but lesbian.**

BS: Do you think they used "Bisexual" Actresses for legal...?

BH: **Yes. It's so all-inclusive. Did you notice the top photo [of three, including Marilyn Monroe and Kristy McNichol] is Joan Crawford?**

BS: Of course I noticed!...It's a very old photo.

BH: **Before this list, in *Mommie Dearest*, it said Crawford had lesbian tendencies...?**

BS: It would have killed Joan to be called lesbic by that daughter of hers. Fortunately for Joan, that was over-looked in the publicity about her being an alleged child-beater. That, she wouldn't have minded as much as the other.

BH: **But that's ridiculous! One is hurting a person—a child—the other is loving or pleasuring a consenting adult.**

BS: I'm talking about Joan, not me. Let's get it over with. What questions?

BH: **Do you think bisexuality was very widespread among female stars during Hollywood's heyday?**

BS: ...I heard that Dietrich, Greta Garbo, most of the girls from Europe, swing either way. Then I found out it's true.

BH: You found out...?

BS: *Next*...!

BH: Next question is...you were good friends with Crawford?

BS: Yes, I was. Next....

BH: But not Bette Davis?

BS: We're not friends, but I admire her as an actress.

BH: Was it very difficult in Hollywood to be a star and not marry? The pressure to wed...?

BS: Personally, I admire the girls who never married. Me, I wouldn't have had the guts! If that's what those gals wanted....

BH: Out of curiosity, I can see what attracted you to Robert Taylor, but what about Frank Fay? [No reply.] Everyone's forgotten he was once a bigger star than you.

BS: He was a bigger star than me. The next question. [Looks at her watch.]

BH: Was there any pressure to wed Robert Taylor?

BS: [Pursed lips.] I don't know about any pressure.

BH: You were the bigger star. It was his first marriage.

BS: I won't say anything about either of his marriages.

BH: No, but there was apparently pressure on him to wed. [No response.] And of course a marriage between two stars generates that much more publicity and can help both careers.

BS: You're curious about the actor's private life?

BH: I know a woman whose husband—a studio executive—is basically heterosexual, but she says he had an affair with Robert Taylor when they were young.

BS: What year?

BH: I didn't ask her. She says it lasted a few months, and the husband never regretted it.

BS: Who is she?

BH: I can't say.

BS: [Rising.] Then don't you dare ask me if it was an arranged marriage! [Notice I didn't ask yet.] I'm damned tired of that impertinent question. Now, please leave.

BH: I'm sorry to have upset you.

BS: Just please get out.

BH: Or if the truth bothers you. I will take the headline and the list with me—thank you. At least you got top billing.... Thank you for your time.

CAPUCINE

(1 9 3 1 – 1 9 9 0)

Before upscale America discovered Catherine Deneuve, France's coolest thespic export was Capucine. She was glacial, angular, and soignée. And needless to say, glamorous. Today she's largely forgotten, for her string of roles revealed little about her, and she didn't stay long enough to join the tinseltown pantheon. Like most Continental actresses, Capucine's Hollywood career lasted a decade or less. Because her allure was based on what one saw and, to a lesser extent, heard, as she neared forty the roles grew fewer and farther between.

She returned to Europe and was seen seldom here, usually on television, where the parts were fleeting, her younger costars overwhelming, and the vehicles instantly forgettable. Capucine's dramatic suicide, jumping from the eighth-floor window of her Swiss attic apartment, caused a mere ripple of recognition in the States. In much of the media, it went unreported, or incorrectly—*Variety* said she did it in Lausanne, *Hollywood Now and Then* placed the suicide in Geneva. One paper wrote that Capucine left behind three cats, another five cats, and one account had her leaping from the fifth floor, another the third (maybe they mixed up the storeys and cats). A motive was not assigned; later reports allowed that the fifty-nine-year old suffered from depression. Insiders believed she was bothered more about her declining finances than her stymied career.

An unnamed source termed her "a lonely lady." No one spoke of her private life. For whom was she lonely? For one in particular? As in life, her death supplied more questions than answers. "She was part Mona Lisa," said director Blake Edwards. "The half-smile. The enigma."

Germaine Lefebvre was born in Toulon, France, in January, 1931, eventually giving her birth year as 1933. She rarely discussed her childhood. By the time she'd reached five feet, seven inches, her grey eyes and haughty cheekbones indicated a living as a fashion model. In her teens, she became a popular model at leading Paris couture houses. Christian Dior recalled, "She had old eyes, her eyes were impervious....She had elegant, flaring nostrils...and seemed to contain a suppressed anger. Above all, she was an ideal mannequin. She wore the clothes well, and her personality did not dominate the clothes. She is beautiful but not a classic. She is too individual to be classical."

Ambitious and restless, she recreated herself as Capucine (pronounced Kap-oo-seen). By twenty, she had wed, but later said so little about the relationship that most of her biographies omitted it. Like such disparate icons as Mae West and Katharine Hepburn, Capucine preferred to be thought of as independently single. "From my youth, already I knew it was my work I would continue with...."

With her prominent, liquid eyes, the young model resembled an early, vulnerable Joan Crawford. By the time she'd become an actress, making her film debut in 1949, she was being dubbed the new Garbo. Capucine made a few more French films, but her impact in such titles as *Frou-Frou* was limited, and in the 1950s, she transferred her modeling career to New York, with its skyscraping salaries.

She next studied with actor-director-coach Gregory Ratoff, best remembered as the dyspeptic producer Max in *All About Eve*. After resituating herself in Hollywood, Capucine made her American film bow in 1960, as a princess in the prestigious flop *Song Without End*, aka Film Without End. The biopic starred Dirk Bogarde as composer Franz Liszt and was unofficially helmed by the gilt-edged George Cukor.

The "woman's director" par excellence offered, "She didn't have much range. Capucine was a Look. Bacall and others were launched as a Look. However, Capucine was rather wooden on screen and inhibited. She *posed*....Movies were her passport and her means, but she put more energy into her life, into traveling and living it up on both continents in between film assignments. That's just what they were to her.

"She never claimed to be an artist."

Producer Charles K. Feldman, who claimed to have discovered Capucine, took her up and pushed her on and off screen. By now she was legally single again, and the media was glad to feed the older man's ego and their own circulation by painting the two as a couple—which boosted her career and his status. Cukor averred, "Capucine had no romantic interest in Mr. Feldman. But she was smart; she let herself be used, and in so doing, used him. She wasn't very talented, so she needed him."

She was next teamed with John Wayne in the lightweight *North to Alaska*, then appeared more at home in the all-star, controversial 1962 movie of the best-selling novel *Walk On the Wild Side*. The then-salacious epic costarred Anne Baxter as a Mexican and Jane Fonda as a hooker named Kitty Twist. Capucine was part of a love triangle also comprising a miscast Laurence Harvey (an Englishman by way of Lithuania) as the Southern antihero and Barbara Stanwyck as Jo, the lesbian madam (with a censorship-Code-mandated husband), both in love with Hallie (Capucine), Jo's fiercely prized best "girl."

Capucine's widest exposure came in the popular *The Pink Panther*, as the wife of Inspector Clouseau (Peter Sellers) who secretly dallies with the larcenous Panther (David Niven). Capucine replaced Ava Gardner in the plum role, but the show was stolen by Sellers, by Claudia Cardinale (another Continental actress with the equivalent of fifteen minutes of Hollywood fame), and by the eponymous cartoon cat. Some two decades later, Capucine returned in two of the series' feeble sequels, *Trail of the Pink Panther* (1982) and *Curse of the Pink Panther* (1984). By then, it was like beating a dead panther.

Following her association with Feldman, Capucine was romantically linked with William Holden, her costar in two little-seen pictures. Because Capucine was contractually single, the press made much of the friendship or romance, proclaiming that the long-married Bill had left his wife for the slinky foreigner. A more serious threat to Holden's marriage to Brenda Marshall had been his affair with the married Audrey Hepburn, which did not make the newspapers. At any rate, Holden returned to his wife—he and Capucine had been on location overseas—but the friendship survived to the extent that in his will the actor bequeathed her fifty thousand dollars.

How serious was Capucine's most publicized relationship? Britisher Oscar Millard, who scripted *Song Without End*, noted, "I knew Bill Holden, we had several friends in common. He was very fond of Capucine and always spoke highly of her. He once stated that she'd done him some great kindness. It may have had to do with his alcoholism, I don't know. When he spoke of her, it was in the same tone as when he spoke of particular actors or directors of whom he was fond or respectful but with whom he certainly was not in love.

"Did they, at some point during shooting together, go to bed with one another? Who can possibly say? And what does it matter? It may have been a romantic though platonic friendship or at one time an affair, but what matters is that they cared about each other and they did stay in touch."

BH: What was it like working with John Wayne?

C: He was very businesslike. It was a John Wayne picture, he knew it, and he expected everyone else to know it. By then he was an institution, in America.

BH: Was he friendly?

C: Not friendly nor aloof. Very involved with himself and those who were attending to him. I had the feeling he was suspicious of me. I can't tell you why. Was he suspicious of all women? Of a European? It is true that many leading men are afraid of being upstaged by their leading lady, even though most leading men have bigger and more scenes, and more dialogue than the actress. Some are afraid that when the leading lady is on the screen, the audience will look at her and not him. Most actors are really very insecure.

BH: Somebody who looks like you probably didn't worry much about people looking at her.

C: You are right. I was more concerned with what I wore. I didn't want to look plain nor overdressed.

BH: **Dirk Bogarde never became a star in America. Were you nervous working with him?**

C: No. Not nervous, a little disappointed. He was chilly, that one. He had more reserve than most of the English have. He was much friendlier with the director [Cukor].

BH: **Might that be because both were gay?**

C: I imagine. Of course, I did not know it at that time.

BH: **Were you nervous working with John Wayne?**

C: No. Of course, I knew my role was window dressing. It was not a splendid role. But what I remember is that he wore lifts—everyone talked about it. And I believe he had a wig or toupee, as well. It surprised me....Years later, when he was in Europe visiting, a friend of mine told me that he [Wayne] was watching a tennis match on television, and he was so involved with it. It was an American player, a girl, against a European, and he was using very strong language and cheering the player he preferred. As if it was his daughter who was playing and booing her opponent.

Afterward, my friend asked him, "Do you know this girl?" and John Wayne said something more vulgar but similar to, "No, I just always want the American to beat the pants off the foreigner."

BH: **A nationalist. Who won?**

C: The tennis match? I don't know. Who cares, really?

BH: **Speaking of political witchhunts, in which Wayne was cheerfully involved, you were directed [in *Walk On the Wild Side*] by Edward Dmytryk, one of the Hollywood Ten, who later recanted. Were you aware of Dmytryk's history when you worked together?**

C: After work, some of use would socialize, or I would go to parties, and they would ask me about him or tell me things about Barbara Stanwyck. She was considered very brave even to accept that role. No one ever said I was brave [laughs], but I was playing the prostitute she was in love with.

BH: **Maybe Hollywood expects anything from a European.**

C: I think so.

BH: **Was the consensus for or against Dymtryk?**

C: I think most felt he was cowardly for what he had done. But this was after the blacklists were officially over, because they ended [in 1960] with *Spartacus* [which gave official credit to blacklisted screenwriter Dalton Trumbo, another of the Hollywood Ten]. For me, I was afraid of politics. Even before I went to America, I was told often that as an outsider I should never give a political opinion, even if asked.

BH: **In those days, stars were never asked for theirs.**

C: It was easier! We all knew that a movie actor's career could be hurt or destroyed if he was of the left. But if he was of the right, it would not hurt him.

BH: **Look at John Wayne or Ward Bond or...**

C: Ronald Reagan.

BH: **What did they tell you about Barbara Stanwyck?**

C: Because she was playing a lesbian?

BH: **Or because she was a lesbian playing a lesbian. Most of the time, gay actors won't play gay roles—like Rock Hudson.**

C: I think actresses are more daring.

BH: **Perhaps they're more daring because a lesbian or bisexual role doesn't hurt a woman's image as much.**

C: That is true, because our roles are usually—when we are young—are involved with sexuality. We are seldom heroines, so we don't have to be virgins. Except if one plays Jeanne d'Arc, where they insist to make her a virgin, but a heterosexual virgin.

BH: **Most history books don't admit that Joan liked to wear men's clothes before she ever led an army.**

C: Yes, well, long ago I read that the Vatican chose to canonize her at the very time when rumors were spreading that Jeanne d'Arc had had a close companion....

BH: **A bosom buddy?**

C: Yes, another girl. Formally, they made her a saint, and that made her seem asexual, and no one would ask any more questions.

BH: **Did you hear, at the time, that Stanwyck was a lesbian?**

C: I heard several things. A few people did say that. But it was such a shocking thing to say then, that few people used the word. I remember one man saying, "Barbara is sapphically inclined."

BH: **How quaint.**

C: *Oui, c'est drôle, ça.* But mostly, they said either that she is "neutral"...

BH: **What would they mean by that?**

C: I think not heterosexual but not homosexual, either.

BH: **Bisexual?**

C: Yes. But not asexual. Bisexual. Other people said they had heard she had a love affair with this woman or that woman.

BH: **Any names?**

C: Yes, one famous name, and a few I didn't recognize. But I don't think I should tell you.

BH: **Because?**

C: She is still alive, Miss Stanwyck....

BH: **Did any rumors or stories link her with other stars you can name?**

C: I tell you two things that I heard. One story, I heard when we were making that picture. From a famous couple, writers—a man and a woman but not married to each other. They said Bette Davis and Barbara Stanwyck hated each other. That it was because when Miss Davis was new to the movies, she was in a picture with Miss Stanwyck [*So Big*, from the novel by lesbian Edna Ferber]. And Miss Stanwyck, she tried to approach Bette Davis, who screamed and said no, no, never. So Barbara Stanwyck was very hurt, especially after Bette Davis became a bigger star.

BH: That's interesting, because I've interviewed Davis, who has nothing good to say about Stanwyck, and I've read where Stanwyck is very cool toward Davis. I know that one reason Bette Davis and Joan Crawford had such a feud was the oft-repeated tale that during Bette's reign at Warners, Joan courted her, and Bette gave her a cold shoulder.

C: I have heard that. But now I tell you something interesting. I also heard that Joan Crawford became an enemy to Marilyn Monroe when Marilyn said no to her. But the other thing about Barbara Stanwyck, I heard it years later while making a movie where *I* played the lesbian [*Fräulein Doktor*, 1968]. I heard that when Barbara and Marilyn did a movie together [*Clash By Night*, 1952], Barbara was very kind to Marilyn, who was new and very insecure. And the two became good friends, but more than that....That is what someone said who worked on their movie.

BH: Did you think it likely?

C: It's very possible.

BH: It's sort of funny that female sex symbols are expected to be versatile or sexually fluid, and we're not often surprised when they have a bisexual side. But with male sex symbols, it's shocking if we hear they even flirted with another man, let alone had one affair.

C: They expect more from a man, but also they give him more restrictions.

BH: So do you think Monroe was bisexual or basically heterosexual with a few female flings thrown in?

C: Who can be positive? It depends how wide is the definition of "bisexuality."

BH: I doubt there's such a person as a fifty-fifty bisexual. I think there's an inherent predisposition toward one gender or the other.

C: In human beings. But in animals—male animals—I think they are ready, like the chimpanzees, to insert it into any other chimpanzee, just for the pleasure or relief.

BH: Yes. But male homosexuality among humans doesn't always include penetration.

C: One can say the same of lesbians! [Smiles.] We were discussing Marilyn Monroe, and in the 1950s, in New York and Hollywood, I heard that she lived with a Russian who was her drama coach [Natasha Lytess] and they were lovers. For a long time, they were inseparable, and she would accompany Marilyn onto her sets and act as her personal director. The men who directed her pictures hated this.

BH: On two levels, I'll bet.

C: So it is possible, if Miss Stanywck became her friend, that they came to an understanding, shall we say. Miss Stanwyck may have become more gentle—she was older by then....At a party, I met Joan Crawford when I was new to Hollywood, and she frightened me. She was very severe, although she was smiling.

BH: **Did she approach you?**

C: Not like that. We were in public. But it is natural to most stars, especially women, to flirt and be charming. She tried to be charming, in the little time we had to talk alone, but I found her very forced.

BH: **I hear she was quite threatened by and antagonistic toward younger actresses.**

C: Well, we did not work together, but I think American actresses feel less competitive with us. When we speak other languages, we have accents, so we cannot play Americans and take those roles away from them.

BH: **You were always cast as an aristocratic European.**

C: There you are. It was a stereotype, but not such a bad stereotype!

BH: **One of your cinematic high points is the opening of *The Pink Panther*, where you're running, escaping from the police, and you enter a building, go up in the empty elevator, and inside you completely change your clothes, shoes, and hat, and when you emerge — cool as a cucumber — you walk right past the waiting policemen.**

C: It was wonderful, now when I look back. It was fun to do it, it was friendly, and it was my most successful film. I was lucky to be a part of it.

BH: **Why do you think most of your films weren't hits?**

C: [Shrugs.] I wish I could tell you. Except, what would it affect now? Possibly if they had made the sequels [to *The Pink Panther*] sooner, as they do now....The ones with William Holden — he was a big star, he had so many successes — but our two movies...nothing. But then I did do one that was popular, *What's New, Pussycat?* I had a rather small role, not one as flashy as Peter Sellers with his long wig or Ursula Andress with her leopard skins, but it was a very famous movie, and the song, too.

BH: *Pussycat* had an all-star cast—you, Sellers, Andress, Peter O'Toole, Romy Schneider, Paula Prentiss,...

C: And Woody Allen.

BH: Right. His first, I think. But unlike *Wild Side*'s all-star cast, this one found its niche.

C: Many stars is no guarantee of success for any movie.

BH: Not to speak ill of the dead, but most costars of Laurence Harvey's have said he was a heel.

C: [Smiles.] I cannot criticize him for wanting to be a star, but he thought it permitted him to be rude to people. I never believed that. I also never believed if I was famous it meant I was extremely gifted. But he did. He did not make mischief with me, although he was not very polite sometimes. But he had words with Jane Fonda, I was told, and I know that Miss Stanwyck shouted at him when she felt he needed to be disciplined.

BH: Did you have a love scene with Stanwyck?

C: Oh, no, not like today. [Airily.] They were just starting then [with gay and lesbian themes], and there was no kissing, anything like that. In Hollywood? [Laughs.] But I would not have minded. Why should I?

BH: Later, when you played lesbian, did you have any qualms about it or about your standing in Hollywood?

C: No, no. Who has standing in Hollywood? The bankers, really. For this picture [*Fräulein Doktor*, aka *The Betrayal*], it was in Europe. I played a doctor [Dr. Saforêt, pronounced Sappho-ray] and it starred Suzy Kendall, the English actress. It was based on the story of a spy named Anna Maria Lesser in World War I.

BH: Rather like the story of Mata Hari.

C: Yes, that was a splendid picture—the one with Garbo. I always heard it was not accurate, but she was divine in it. As in everything.

BH: **As in *Queen Christina*, which was even less accurate—it featured a lesbian or bisexual actress playing a lesbian monarch [not a queen consort], but as a heterosexual character.**

C: As they say, it's Hollywood.

BH: **That's Hollywood....In Hollywood, did the studio or your agent ever send you out on an arranged publicity date?**

C: Oh, of course. Like every other actress who ever worked in Hollywood, there came a time when the studio arranged a so-called date for me, and it was with a homosexual actor.

BH: **Not Rock Hudson, by any chance?**

C: No, he was just one....But he was uncomfortable, I was uncomfortable, only the photographers were comfortable. And, of course, the publicity department.

BH: **...Did you have a crush on Garbo?**

C: Of course. You?

BH: ***Mais oui.* I think that the 1930s yielded the most beautiful and glamorous actresses [she nods], Europeans with a universal appeal.**

C: Garbo and Dietrich.

BH: **Yes. Women who appealed to men and women and who apparently acted on their appeal to both men and women.**

C: Which one can say openly even in print in Europe.

BH: **It's been printed in numerous American books I've read about Dietrich. About her bisexuality.**

C: In Hollywood they think all European actresses are lesbian anyway. Or bisexual.

BH: **They never want to say "lesbian," though, about any beautiful actress.**

C: [Smiles.] I think they write more about Dietrich because she has had a husband and child and many affairs with men, too. I think Garbo is more the lesbian, and because she never married, they are more careful what they write about her, though I'm positive she would not sue.

BH: **It's my experience that most homosexual stars don't dare sue, for fear of magnifying the truth.**

C: It's also more common for Americans to sue. Here, what do we care what the farmers in Kansas or Oklahoma think?

BH: **Let them get used to it.**

C: About me, they have already said so many things, I cannot begin to tell you. That was before. But if they say anything about you, it means they are interested. In a way, it is worse when they say nothing about you.

The most outrageous rumor about Capucine was that she was actually a transsexual. This made its way into print in *The Hollywood Death Book* in 1992 (somewhere along the way, Mae West and singer Donna summer were believed to be male transvestites). Hollywood columnist Lee "Man About Town" Graham once wrote that Capucine had been discovered to be a second cousin to Barbra Streisand. "Come to think of it, Capucine's nose does resemble la Streisand's, though a junior version."

Following the hit *What's New, Pussycat?*, Capucine's tinseltown star began to fade fast. Her next assignment was promising and prestigious but hurt a number of screen careers. *The Honey Pot* was writer-director Joseph L. Mankiewicz's adaptation of *Volpone*. A multiple Oscar winner, Mankiewicz had shaped such projects as *A Letter to Three Wives*, *All About Eve*, *Suddenly, Last Summer*, and *Cleopatra*. *Honey Pot* (1967) starred Rex Harrison, relatively fresh from his triumphs in *Cleopatra* and *My Fair Lady* (an Oscar as Henry Higgins).

Capucine's female costars were Susan Hayward and Edie Adams. One scene found Hayward, playing a brittle Texan called Lone Star, dressing down the patrician Capucine and the middle-American Adams. She warned the former, "Hold on to your hat, Highness," and the latter, "You too, Lowness...." Shot partly in Venice, the lavishly budgeted film also featured but didn't hurt Cliff Robertson and Maggie Smith.

After that, it was back to European films, including the sapphic turn in *Fräulein Doktor* which set Hollywood tongues to openly wagging ("I told you so," was the dominant refrain). Capucine confessed in *Paris Match*, "By then, I did not care. I knew how fickle was the public, and the film makers in Los Angeles....I knew it was a better film than most I had made there, and I knew it would close most doors to me in Hollywood, which as far as I was concerned were already shut or closing."

She had long since realized that "I could not carry a picture." Rarely was she the de-facto leading lady, and now she resigned herself to glamorous support. "If the part is interesting and the money as well, why not? I am not a dedicated actress à la Bernhardt, I am an ex-model. But when they invite me, I prefer to say thank you, yes."

Her next two were European hits: the dazzlingly unique *Fellini Satyricon* (1969) in which she played a rich Roman named Tryphaena who takes a bisexual hunk in hand, and the all-star *Red Sun* (1971) with Alain Delon, Ursula Andress, Charles Bronson, and Toshiro Mifune. But then came the

Continental nonhits with names like *Exquisite Cadaver*, the unfinished *Jackpot*, the flop *Panther* sequels, and a flurry of activity in 1982: five movies, including supporting rather than playing *Aphrodite*. Further down the line, Capucine accepted guest shots on American television in such series as "Hart to Hart" and "Murder, She Wrote" and telefilms like *Sins* and *Blue Blood*.

She gave her final performance in 1989 in *My First Forty Years*. In 1988 an Italian newspaper complained, "Is there no better use to make of singular and enduringly beautiful actresses 'of a certain age' than casting them as aunts or countesses and wasting the mystique and exciting presence of stars like Capucine and Gina Lollobrigida?"

After wrapping a "Murder, She Wrote" in 1985, Capucine was staying with friends in Paris, and I got to interview her in a "guest office" of the majestic city hall. Previously, I'd requested an interview upon release of her third *Panther*, but she did few interviews to publicize the film (she may well have guessed its fate). When Capucine telephoned my hotel to confirm the time and place of our meeting, she casually insisted, "This is not to make publicity for "Murder, She Wrote." I know it is quite popular, but it would be ridiculous to make a big fuss for this, although I was happy to be on the show."

In person—accompanied by a fortyish female friend whom she introduced as "my part-time secretary"—Capucine wore what I took for Chanel, in beige and brown. Plus a signature turban hat, black to match her shoes. Only the gloves were missing. A bit frail-looking but elegant and very together, she seemed emotionally detached from her past, yet unenthusiastic about the present or future.

Whenever a comment struck her companion as amusing, it was reflected on Capucine's face. Her manner turned more serious and almost nervous—now speaking more in English than French—after the other woman excused herself about halfway through the interview. But it was then that we pursued more personal topics.

BH: **Did you enjoy modeling?**

C: It was a very easy way to make a living. But work is work—you have to be there.

BH: **Was it flattering or boring?**

C: ...You know, both!

BH: **Were you ever surprised how far you went as an actress? Most models don't succeed in films.**

C: I was surprised. I kept thinking, "But when will they see that I am really decorative?"

BH: **An actress can be both decorative and talented.**

C: She can be. She is better off not to be too decorative.

BH: **Like who?**

C: Bette Davis. She had a difficult time becoming known, but then she stayed and stayed. Because of talent.

BH: **And personality. And determination!**

C: Yes, but when one has no looks to lose, the change—the transition—to older roles is easier.

BH: **Davis was underrated in the looks department, early on, don't you think?**

C: Oh, yes. She was ravishing, very often. But she was lucky they did not write mostly about how she looked. They were not impressed how she looked. She was very lucky.

BH: **What was it like working with Fellini?**

C: I think for my part he wanted Jacqueline Kennedy. Before he made his *Satyricon*, he announced all the famous people he wanted to have in it. He got none of them. It had no stars. I was the biggest star in it, I think. As usual, Fellini was the star.

BH: It could have used more of you.

C: Thank you. I think so, too.

BH: To go back one moment, did you ever have a career drive or ambition as Herculean as Bette Davis's?

C: ...Somebody said that she said that she never became sad, only angry. If she had a disappointment, it made her more angry. More determined. Not me. I become sad, or I avoid having a confrontation. I could not argue with a director or producer.

BH: Because he's a man?

C: Men always want to win arguments against women. I didn't have that strength or energy. And I was also from another country, so always I felt like a guest.

BH: Do you think the biggest, longest-lasting actresses are, to coin a phrase, ball busters?

C: [Laughs softly.] I think they have to have more anger than tears. [Shrugs dejectedly.]

BH: What about the sequels to *The Pink Panther*?

C: I did them for old times' sake and for the money. I was asked.

BH: What did you think when William Holden died alone?

C: Some people who drink become terrible people. He never did. He was a very nice man. It was tragic.

BH: But how could a star as big as he die in such a lonely way? [He fell while drunk and gashed his head on a table corner, then bled to death in his apartment where he was discovered days later]. According to the press, he was outgoing, friendly, he had friends and was very close to Stephanie Powers [to whom he also bequeathed money]. Yet it took days until he was missed.

C: You know, people each have their own lives, their schedules. It is so easy to be involved in one's own little world. Bill was sociable, but I think as he drank more, he let go of several of his friends. He hated getting older. [Shrugs.] Perhaps he was sad or unhappy about his career.

BH: **But aging male stars have less to be unhappy about. The wrinkles don't stop the roles. He was well into middle age when he did films like *Network* and *S.O.B.* for Blake Edwards and in leading roles.**

C: Alcoholism....[Shakes head.] I don't know.

BH: **Were you in love with him?**

C: I loved him. At one time, very much.

BH: **Did you resent media coverage of your relationship?**

C: Yes. He was married, and they made it as though it were illicit. Like something...naughty.

BH: **Did they misrepresent it?**

C: You mean did they make it sordid? [Muses.] That is an English word which sounds like what it means.

BH: **Did they make it sexual?**

C: Ah....He desired me more than I desired him. That is the truth. I cherished his friendship all my life. He was much more than an actor, and he wanted to be more. He was very far from Hollywood, and I admired that.

BH: **Literally, too, with homes in Hong Kong and East Africa.**

C: He wanted to be part of the wider world than just Hollywood. Most stars don't care about the real world.

BH: **What made him drink? He had so much going for him.**

C: [Shrugs slowly.] I can tell you what made him drink more. It was when his [drunk] driving killed a man. In Italy [in 1966; charged with manslaughter, Holden received a suspended sentence]. It went from bad to worse. He was very guilty.

BH: **Do you think the press was presumptuous in depicting you and Charles Feldman as a pair?**

 C: What is social, they want to make seem sexual. But that is always how Hollywood is. If I went there today and I went to a nightclub with a friend of a friend, and it was a man, and if they took a photograph, they would write it [the caption] as if we were dating or lovers. [Laughs slightly.] They can think what they like, I no longer worry.

BH: **Oscar Wilde once said, or it was attributed to him, that nothing looks so innocent as an indiscretion. This readily applies to the media. For instance, if a lesbian actress goes out with her girlfriend, and they take along the girlfriend's brother, the resulting photographs will picture the actress with the male and probably leave her girlfriend out altogether.**

 C: No, or they will say that the actress brought her date, who brought his sister.

BH: **If they check the identities at all.**

 C: It is, it is like a conspiracy.

BH: **And when someone famous dies who was gay or lesbian, unless that star was very flamboyant or died of AIDS, their sexual orientation is still hidden from the public.**

 C: Especially if there is a wife who remains, or a husband.

BH: **Or children.**

 C: Yes, they [the media] want everyone to think people are all alike.

BH: **Diversity is feared. Particularly if it's sexual or religious.**

 C: Yes. Now they accept more colors, but not a different way to love or believe.

BH: **Why did you marry?**

 C: [Laughs.]...He proposed....But really it was not anything important.

BH: **Was it partly to conform? Or to leave home?**

  C: Oh, you know, if you ask me, "Have you been married?" I can say, with my honest opinion, "Not really."

BH: **What about ever married—to whoever—in the sense of oneness, as opposed to a legal contract?**

  C: [Smiles warmly, briefly.] I have been in love, more than once. But how can I talk about it, even if I should?

BH: **Because of your career or image?**

  C: No, no, no. Not that. [Grins.] Because, you see, if it is a private life, how can one talk about it in public? More so if it will be published.

BH: **Hollywood sees no contradiction in publicly dissecting private lives.**

  C: But Hollywood is its own self a contradiction.

BH: *Touché.* **Why did you leave him?**

  C: Oh...I grew up.

BH: **It's not a subject you're keen on.**

  C: It has nothing to do with me now.

BH: **A contractual marriage remains on one's record forever.**

  C: *Malheureusement.* But you know, in those days, you could not experiment, to see how it was, how one felt. It was marriage or no.

BH: **In Hollywood, was there ever pressure on you to marry?**

  C: No. Thank heaven. I might have left Hollywood....

BH: **Was there no pressure because you'd already married or because you were publicized *vis-à-vis* some famous men?**

  C: Because of both, I think.

BH: **At one point, it seemed as if William Holden was going to divorce his wife for you.**

  C: That would not have happened. [Firmly.]

BH: **Did you ever fall in love in Hollywood?**

  C: No...not really. There are beautiful people there. One can have a big crush. That is not love.

BH: **As a busy actress in the 1960s, did you have time for much of a private life?**

C: Everyone has time for a private life. That is nonsense, when someone says they are too busy with work to have a private life. Or to be married or whatever. No one works all the time, and for actors, most of one's time is in between making movies. There is time for whatever is important to you.

BH: **Then there are those actresses who declare that having a career prevents them from having a successful marriage.**

C: No. [Shakes head.] To be together is not the measure of success in a relationship. Everything depends on the individual. Some people are happier if they are apart much of the time, not stuck together.

BH: **And others crave togetherness.**

C: But with most actors or actresses, it is the career that really comes first. Although no one will say this out loud....It all depends on the individual. Mostly, what ruins a famous actress's marriage is when the man feels he cannot control her or at least meet her as an equal. Men don't like to be gigolos, unless they are being paid —well paid.

BH: **What about the actress who says that her career prevents her having children?**

C: Instead, she might say, "I don't want children. Why should I?"

BH: **Women aren't supposed to say that.**

C: [Impatient.] Well, most women do what they are told. And for rich people, they hire servants to take care of the children. Royalty does this, the rich people in Hollywood and everywhere else, also. But they hide it. Money makes someone very different from those without much money.

BH: **Yet the rich always wish to seem similar to the middle class.**

C: Especially in America! It is funny when a star who earns millions of dollars for one movie says in an interview that he leads an average life.

BH: **When you married, was it average?**

C: Honestly, I don't remember.

BH: **May I ask what is rather a crude question?**

C: You can ask.

BH: **When a beautiful actress is the protégée of a powerful agent or producer, does he always demand sexual favors in return?**

C: [Smiles.] Charlie was heterosexual—not all of them are. Usually, of course, they want something in return. But if a girl is alert to how things are, she knows that he is benefiting, too. His reward is not just her company, but being thought virile and able to attract somebody young and beautiful and perhaps famous. Most men, I think, value that—what others think of them—more than they do an act of sex which they can get elsewhere or buy.

BH: **Cold reality.**

C: It is men who are cold. They almost never give as much as they take. Not just in Hollywood.

BH: **Did numerous men seek your company in Hollywood?**

C: [Waves hand dismissively.] Oh! You see, when a man like that promotes an actress, he is hoping she will make much money for him. So he needs her on his side. Even if there is a business contract, he cannot offend her too much. In a way, they are business partners, and she is the one on the screen, not him. So he is not in complete control, at all.

BH: **It sounds like you had a shrewd head for business.**

C: Because I was lucky enough to earn good money from modeling, and if you earn money, you either become smart or foolish from it. At heart, I am a good *bourgeoise*. When I was very young, I saved and planned, and in Hollywood, too.

BH: **For an actress, you started at a pretty late age in Hollywood.**

C: Yes, I was not even near eighteen or twenty then. It hurt me—my career there. They prefer to see you growing up. Before they turn their backs on you. [Smiling coolly.]

BH: **Also, don't male producers and audiences prefer the vulnerability of an actress in her twenties?**

C: By thirty, she has formed into an adult.

BH: **And by forty?**

C: Well, it is better now. I began at almost thirty, and in the old days, long ago, by thirty an actress was thought rather old. By forty, she could retire or play smaller parts. Now, in their forties, many actresses look very good. So what was once forty, now it is fifty.

BH: **Do you think being perceived as cool or icy hurt your career?**

C: [Grins.] Yes, it did....Look at Doris Day. Or Betty Grable. The ones who are like their girlfriends—the sweet ones—they like them the best.

BH: **What about the blonde factor?**

C: I think for an American it helps her. But most of the European actresses, we were not blonde. From Garbo and Dietrich, and Loren...other Italians. You see, blondes are not exotic. To be available, that is not so exotic.

BH: **Brunettes are less attainable?**

C: European brunettes. But because we seem not attainable, we were also less popular. Now, when everyone wants more sex and women so available, the Europeans are not popular in Hollywood anymore. Actresses or actors. Now, they only want Americans.

BH: **Ironically, it's a less international outlook today.**

C: If I was young and went to Hollywood now, I would not have the opportunities I had.

BH: **Did bad reviews ever hurt your feelings, or is that a dumb question?**

C: No. I did not read them.

BH: **Some thespians say they learn from reviews.**

C: I don't believe it. And I didn't want to be self-conscious. In America, when they write about actors, they are very personal, sometimes cruel. I knew I looked good, but also I knew there is always another actress who is more beautiful, more young....If I was in a movie and it was popular, then I said to myself, "Well done." For what the critics? [Shrugs.]

BH: **For the masochism, I guess. Did any of your leading men proposition you?**

C: But not to talk about William Holden anymore....Good. Well, a few. It cannot be helped. If one works in an office and the man comes to you and says, "Let's go to bed," you have a right to slap him, and he is wrong. But if you work with a man doing a scene kissing, embracing, or in bed, and when it is done, he says, "Let's go to bed," you cannot blame him. You either say no...or perhaps yes.

BH: **Did any actresses proposition you?**

C: [Laughs.] Ah....That happens, too.

BH: **How does an actress's approach differ from an actor's?**

C: [Smiles widely.] If it is two women, she doesn't ask in public—in front of the others.

BH: **Women have the advantage of being able in public to be physical or affectionate with each other.**

C: Yes. But we never have love scenes together. So it would have been more difficult for another actress to make the transition from a conversation about a man [in a scene] to telling you that your hair is wonderful and can you come visit me in my dressing room?

BH: **Difficult but not impossible. Who asked you?**

C: Perhaps I did the asking....

BH: **Yes?**

C: Really, I don't want to disappoint you. Also, I don't want to lie. Miss Stanwyck did not flirt with me — I'm not sure if even she liked me, she was very businesslike. I think at that time, she had a lady friend, and she was not looking for someone else. And being such a big star, so known to everybody in Hollywood, she would have to be very careful. In her place, I also would not take chances. I heard that most of her close friends were not actresses.

On the set, I was never propositioned by an actress. When an actress, or someone's wife, or any girl was interested, it was brought up socially, away from my work. At parties or lunch, shopping, at somebody's house, or on vacation....Women are more discreet in making themselves known.

BH: **Would you have married in Hollywood for money?**

C: A man? No. I wanted money, but to earn it. Not to...be like a slave, with my name changed to his. His identity. His money, like an allowance to a child....I never married for money. I still never would, irregardless.

BH: **Did you have any affair, an ongoing relationship, with a famous woman, actress or not?**

C: Have you heard something about me? [Leans forward.]

BH: **Not much. You remain a woman of mystery.**

C: [Leans back, reclining.] Good. It's better.

BH: **Do you like the word "lesbian"?**

C: It doesn't repel me, but it sounds like a nationality. And if you say "homosexual," it sounds like for men only. For women, there should be another word.

BH: Like "sapphic"?

C: [Grimaces.] Well,...I don't see the need for labels and categories.

BH: There is no need. But people do label and categorize, and everyone fits into a number of categories—like left-handed or heterosexual or blue-eyed....

C: But I think if one is considered sexual or not sexual, it is enough.

BH: So you wouldn't call yourself heterosexual?

C: Oh, *I* wouldn't. But if the publicity people would see a need to say that, I don't care.

BH: Even if it's not true?

C: Most publicity is not true.

BH: Most people are sexual, period. It's really acts, not people, that are hetero- or homosexual.

C: Most Americans think it's either 100 percent heterosexual or 100 percent homosexual. It's much more complex than that. Look at ancient Greece.

BH: Right. The ancient Greeks didn't have words for being only what is now called gay or straight.

C: I know there have been many rumors about me, but few people ask me questions about this. [Smiles.]

BH: Perhaps they fear the answers—if, that is, they expect the truth from a performer doing publicity for the mass public.

C: Yes. It is very foolish when they make an interview with a famous star, and then they ask her or him, "Are you gay?"

BH: It is, in light of society's and Hollywood's homophobia. Who's going to willingly make themselves an object of contempt?

C: Or possibly a boycott.

BH: **And yet things can only change when gays and lesbians— and bisexuals—come out of invisibility.**

C: What is worst about invisibility is that it allows the majority to define the minority and to use stereotypes against it, and lies.

BH: **No one wants to be categorized, but it's better to categorize oneself than have others do it. Who was that—I'm sure he was French—writer who said that it's better to be disliked for who one is than liked for what one is not?**

C: It sounds like Sartre. He made so much good publicity for [gay writer] Jean Genêt, that he finished by calling him Saint Genêt.

BH: **That's rather ludicrous because Genêt was in most ways a very negative personality and full of prejudices. The fact of somebody's sexual orientation is neither good nor bad.**

C: As you said, it is like being left-handed or right-handed.

BH: **And there have been many more positive famous gays and lesbians than Genêt to publicize. Who knows what Sartre intended?**

C: You know, not that it bothers me, but in America one hears or reads so much about gay people and gay rights, but it is very much about and for the *men*.

BH: **Why doesn't it bother you?**

C: I don't let it. There is always injustice. Especially against women.

BH: **I'm a feminist. Are you?**

C: If you are, I am. [Smiles.]

BH: **Anyone who isn't anti-women is a feminist. Are you for lesbian rights?**

C: Of course.

BH: **Would it bother you to be called lesbian?**

C: No. The word, I don't like. But I don't hate men....

BH: **That's one of the myths or lies—that because one doesn't want to have sex with a gender, one hates that gender.**

C: The ones who hate women are mostly the men who abuse their wives or girlfriends.

BH: **Or daughters. Do you miss not having had children? Admittedly a sexist question.**

C: Always they want to know about an actress's life or an actor's work. They didn't ask about my directors, they would ask if I found my leading man attractive or fell in love with him? [Giggles.] To answer your question, I did not miss what I never had. [Shakes head emphatically.]

BH: **How did you deal with silly questions about your costars?**

C: I did it easily—I didn't give interviews. Not if I could avoid it.

BH: **Do you ever miss being interviewed or being the center of a publicity campaign, and all the photographs?**

C: [Smiles.] I don't know if I was ever the center of a campaign, but yes, one misses the attention. Not the photographs—not at my age—but yes, the interviews. Now that I'm older, the questions are better. Or maybe you are a better interviewer.

BH: **Or the times have evolved, and actresses are treated as if they have brains.**

C: And pocketbooks! *Mon Dieu....* Now, when they earn millions and some of them have a great control over their projects....

BH: **Do you feel good for them?**

C: Oh, yes. I envy them, but I don't hate them. Good for them! When I was in Hollywood, I saw so often how even famous actresses could be treated like prostitutes, if they did not value themselves. Men are always ready to dominate women.

BH: It's like kids—they'll go as far as they're allowed or encouraged to go. What created your self-esteem?

C: Well,...I knew I was in demand. I knew what they were willing to pay me. And I knew that I could never think of myself as a person who was here in life just to be a part of some man's life or his world.

BH: Were you ever exclusively heterosexual?

C: But you see, mostly I have not been sexual. It may not be true for men, but I think a woman can be hetero or homo without being sexual most of the time. It sounds strange, all these labels: homo, hetero, bi.

BH: How about pansexual or polysexual, which means the same as bi?

C: But why sexual at all? Yes, I have had romantic or sexual liaisons with women, and one or two with men. But it was with an individual, one person, and usually when it happened, it was because I was so strongly attracted. It was unique. Each time.

BH: You're not very sexual, then?

C: Then or now.

BH: You know, I think most people, most of the time, are autosexual....

C: Oh...self-pleasure. Well, yes. There is often that, especially when one is younger.

BH: What is the difference between a romantic or a sexual relationship with another woman? [No reply.] When it's romantic, does that mean no sex or a little?

C: It means sex is not the main thing, or the first or the last thing. With all men, I think, sex is the main thing. When a woman is with a man, in or out of bed, she has to conform more to what he is. When a woman is alone or with another, she can be herself. Sometimes it's more difficult alone, sometimes with another because one must make the effort of compromise. But in relationships of most kinds, I feel more comfortable with women. Only except in business.

BH: **Who have you loved most in your life?**

C: Now you ask too much. No names. Not because of you; it's the principle. What is splendid and special is for one or two people. It might be discussed, a little bit, with people one knows very well. But it is not for interviews.

BH: **I can appreciate that, of course. Do you think if you were in Hollywood today, starting out or already a star, you would be more open about your orientation?**

C: Ah [raises a forefinger]...but I was not hiding it. I never said I was what I was not. And they [other actresses] still do say that.

BH: **And they say it in the same way: by consistently going out with members of the opposite sex....**

C: The other sex. People are not so opposite.

BH: **...Or by being romantically linked in the media with famous actors or executives.**

C: Everyone does that. But what was different is I was never asked, in that time or place, "Are you this or are you that?"

BH: **No, because it was assumed, and hoped, that everyone was sexually alike.**

C: I would never have wanted to deny being different, but you know, again I was lucky. Being French, I was already very different in their eyes. So if I was more aloof from men, if I was not a *maman* [mother], it was because I was Continental. But it is true, when I came back to Europe, I felt less pressure, and it was easier for me to meet women because we speak the same language and we are not so competitive; the women in Hollywood are as competitive as the men, and just as untrustworthy. I found it very difficult to ever confide in a woman there. They wanted your body or your fame or something else. Always they wanted something from you. To take, not to give. Just like men.

BH: Were you ever, perhaps as a girl, abused by men? Or a man?

C: A man? No. Only by men — in the ordinary ways.

BH: Have the true loves of your life been women?

C: Yes. [Coughs.]

BH: Do you ever miss Hollywood?

C: Oh...sometimes I miss the lifestyle, the *éclat*. I miss my youth!

BH: You're still fabulous-looking.

C: *Oh, non! Merci!* [Somewhat embarrassed.] Thank you. But I'm not in demand, you see. One misses that. Not just for the money — I have probably talked too much about money. Whereas in Hollywood, they only *think* of money....

BH: How do you want to be remembered?

C: I really don't care if people do. What good would it do me when I'm not here? I like to try and enjoy it while I am here.

To "try and enjoy." Only those close to her knew that Capucine suffered from depression and fatigue, chronic or otherwise. A few years before her death, she informed a reporter, "I'm weary, always weary, these days. I'd like to work, but the enthusiasm is gone. But then, so are the opportunities."

The end came in winter, 1990, less than five years after our interview (the secretary, who seemed more like a friend than an assistant, never did return; perhaps she'd dropped Capucine off at the Hôtel de Ville and then sat in our session until satisfied that things were going well).

I attempted to find out through relatives of mine near Zürich what were the circumstances of Capucine's final years. She lived alone, save for her cats, but was she close to anyone, did she have friends? Was she a recluse? Was she ill? Their inquiries went unanswered, and the typical posthumous for-publicity comments by colleagues were few—in Hollywood, almost nonexistent—and centered on a younger Capucine's looks or glamour.

Frederico Fellini stated, "She had a face to launch a thousand ships...but she was born too late." Perhaps too late to join the celluloid pantheon of Euro-goddesses, but Capucine was born too early to benefit from an improving social and professional climate less alarmed by female autonomy and diversity.

SANDY DENNIS

(1 9 3 7 – 1 9 9 2)

As with Rock Hudson, Sandy Dennis was already a friend before I formally interviewed her, more than once. I met her through Robert La Guardia, author of a Monty Clift biography. Then director Robert Moore invited me to Sunday brunch, and there she was. "You *know* each other!" he exclaimed. "But everyone in New York does — in the movies." Moore had known Dennis since helming *The Boys in the Band* on Broadway. "She came up to me, congratulated me, and said she was only sorry she couldn't be in the cast, because of her sex."

There was of course the sex part. Some friends but mostly associates said Sandy Dennis was basically asexual. One actress friend changed her mind; "I used to say she was neutral about sex. But I've since come out, myself." One newspaper claimed that Dennis had wed musician

246 / HOLLYWOOD LESBIANS

Gerry Mulligan in 1975, and they'd separated the next year. Dennis herself insisted that she and Mulligan, who'd reportedly lived together as best friends, never married. Even *People* magazine couldn't unearth a marriage certificate. (Mulligan had also been close to Judy Holliday, who was lesbian or bi and had one marriage and one child, before.)

"I don't know where these things come from," said an ex-publicist. "Sandy doesn't give them out. Either the publications themselves create a boyfriend out of a friend or marry her off, or they get it from some anonymous source who wants Sandy to seem more everyday."

Dennis also reportedly lived for a while with actor Eric Roberts, elder brother of superstar Julia Roberts. Actor Pat McWilliams notes, "I stayed with Sandy a week while my place in Manhattan was being redone. She was fun, her cats were fun, but then I read an item in a column saying that Sandy Dennis's latest 'live-in love' is a struggling young actor she's taken under her wing! I never showed the item to Sandy, but I know it wasn't the first time it happened.

"She had another actor, a guy I know, who stayed with her part of each summer, two, three years in a row. The press made it read like he'd been living two or three years with Sandy Dennis and it was a big romance."

Costar Richard Burton called Sandy "one of the most genuine eccentrics I know of." Her primary trait was humor rather than model looks or conventional femininity. Also talent, for despite her quirkiness and amusing (to some, irritating) mannerisms, she appeared to good effect in numerous dramatic roles on stage and screen. But her unusualness and her remaining legally single made some of her friends and much of the media cover up for her. "When I was in my lesbian movie," she told *Film Monthly*, "I was linked with men I didn't even know!"

Time, sexism, and weight removed Sandy from the spot-light to background roles. British critic David Quinlan wrote, "After five years at the top, it seemed that the public tired of her. But in the studio days, she would have probably been built into a major female star along Bette Davis lines." Dennis informed *People*, "I should have kept myself blonder and thinner, but I just didn't care enough."

She was born Sandra Dale Dennis in Hastings, Nebraska, "land of endless conformity," as she put it. As an actress, she would stand out; in Nebraska, she stood way out. She attended high school with Dick Cavett and at nineteen moved to New York, where she joined the Actors Studio and worked off-Broadway.

In 1961 she made her film bow in a bit part in *Splendor in the Grass*, starring Natalie Wood and Warren Beatty. Her individuality served her better on the stage. She won two Tony awards, in 1963 and '64, for *A Thousand Clowns* and *Any Wednesday*. Predictably, the film versions starred more pasteurized actresses, Barbara Harris and Jane Fonda.

In 1966 Dennis made her official movie debut in the film of Edward Albee's play *Who's Afraid of Virginia Woolf?* The quadripartite cast was nominated for Academy Awards in leading and supporting categories. Elizabeth Taylor and Sandy Dennis won, Richard Burton and George Segal didn't. (Dennis declined to attend the ceremonies.) In 1967 Sandy made her starring movie debut in *Up the Down Staircase* and attained the cover of *Time*, which read "The Star in the $7 Dress."

Her starring career was brief but memorable. So were some of her thespic reviews. Pauline Kael wrote that she "has made an acting style of post-nasal drip." Others stressed her speech patterns—one said she issued each line in triplicate, another that her sentences were like a child who returns to the curb three times before finally crossing the street.

Her films included *The Out-of-Towners* with Jack Lemmon, *Come Back to the Five and Dime, Jimmy Dean, Jimmy Dean* with Cher and Karen Black, *Nasty Habits* — a Watergate satire set in a nunnery with Glenda Jackson in the Nixon role — the lesbian drama *The Fox, Sweet November, That Cold Day in the Park*, and supporting roles in such as *The Four Seasons, 976-EVIL*, and *God Told Me To*.

Most of her 1970s performances were on stage, and in the eighties she worked less, period, with occasional film parts, i.e. a small, blowsy, and unsympathetic one in Woody Allen's *Another Woman* (1988) starring Gena Rowlands (blonde and thin), and Sean Penn's *The Indian Runner* (1991).

I visited Sandy's home in Westport, Connecticut, a few times, and whenever we met in New York, I took us to lunch at the Algonquin or Oscar's at the Waldorf. We didn't meet in person after 1990. Did she know then that she had the ovarian cancer which would claim her at fifty-four in 1992? Some of her friends had already died, others had fallen out of touch, not by their own choice. She'd apprised *People*, "I'm a solitary person," and with time she became more so, retreating inside her cozy home where she left three dogs and twenty-nine cats behind.

BH: You were born in Hastings?

SD: Hastings, yes, that's...yes.

BH: A coincidence: Judy Holliday is buried in Hastings-on-Hudson, New York.

SD: Have you...been to that cemetery? What's it called?

BH: Not yet. I'd like to. It's Westchester Hills Cemetery. The Gershwin brothers are also there.

SD: I had some sad news the other day. Another dancer friend....I guess, um, they used to call themselves chorus boys. He died...of AIDS.

BH: **I'm very sorry. So many dancers....I was watching a 1950s Rosalind Russell movie, *The Girl Rush*, and all those male dancers, some so good-looking you wonder why they didn't become actors or stars. One kind of did, George Chakiris. But several have since died, usually of AIDS.**

SD: Ow, it's, it's so...sad, so depressing.

BH: **We'll change the subject. Someone asked me about an actor friend of yours, a former costar. Wanted to know if he's gay.**

SD: [After I name X.] Ow! Is he...um, I don't know. I wouldn't know. You'd have to ask a *man* that. I mean, he never said he was, and maybe if I was a man, I'd know...you know, if he made goo-goo eyes at me or something. [Smiles.]

BH: **Do non-gay men make goo-goo eyes at you?**

SD: [Laughs.] No! No, not then, and they don't now. No one did, knock wood....I saw this show, and they asked this woman if her ex-husband was gay, and she said no.

BH: **Like anyone ever says otherwise.**

SD: The funniest thing is, she said, "He was never gay around *me*." She was so funny, because of course he wouldn't be! Not around *her*. With a *man*....

BH: **Take a bisexual woman, say.**

SD: Do I have to? [Mock-groans.]

BH: **You're cute. But her husband will swear, from his point of view, that she's hetero. And her female lover, from her perspective, will say the woman's lesbian.**

SD: They're *both* right, aren't they, because that lady is both. Each is a part of her.

BH: **How big a part of your makeup is or was sexuality?**

SD: Ow, that's embarrassing! I always thought, well...sex is okay if you don't talk about it too much. If you turn the lights off. You can always try and sweep it under the rug. You don't have to display it on the mantelpiece.

BH: **The media sure does.**

SD: You've never much asked me about my career....

BH: **Of course I have! [She giggles.] But let's see. *Come Back to the Five and Dime, Jimmy Dean, Jimmy Dean*—whew!—was on TV a few months ago. Do you think your character was very naive, stating she got pregnant by Jimmy Dean?**

SD: You...because he was gay?

BH: **Or bi.**

SD: Robert Altman didn't....We talked about that *after* it was released. All that interest in the eighties in James Dean and...what made him tick....She'd have had egg on her face if she said she got pregnant by a star, and then someone else said, "But he's gay." Then they'd *know* she was lying. But, yes, they didn't bring it up...in the movie.

BH: **They just let most viewers assume Dean was heterosexual. His *Giant* costar, Rock Hudson...**

SD: [Giggling.] Giant? He was...?

BH: **Very funny. Yes. But his costar in *Giant*, Rock Hudson, didn't believe in bisexuals. He was adamant.**

SD: Ow! I've got to ask you a few questions about that *Conversations* book of yours!

BH: **Are you sure? Well, fire away.**

SD: You know the Woolworth's heir? I knew one of his distant...relatives, and I always heard he was *gay*....

BH: **Ah. Jimmy Donahue. Friend of the Duke and Duchess of Windsor. They had a publicist, Russell Birdwell, famous** for publicizing *Gone With The Wind*. It seems Donahue had a fling with the Duke—who was often rumored bisexual and was publicly homophobic to cover his tracks, I guess. Word got out that hanky-panky was occurring. Birdwell couldn't deny it effectively, so he turned it around, saying that yes, Donahue was having an affair—with the Duchess of Windsor.

SD: Ow! Really?! *That's* what it was.

BH: He didn't publicly announce it about Donohue and the duchess, he just put it about.

SD: To deflect...yes, to put everyone on a false scent. They do that, they do. So *that's* it!

BH: Anything else before we...

SD: Yes, yes, hold on. Yes. Oh...where you said about the movie *Exodus* and Israel....You said you always thought the English were "more civilized." Than who?

BH: I meant that we grew up with this image of the British being more polite and fair than other European powers. Then you read about Israel's history and learn that the Brits tried to prevent Jewish survivors of concentration camps from landing in what the empire people named Palestine, and it's a whole other picture.

SD: You mean Otto Preminger's?

BH: Well, *Exodus* depicted part of it. But I mean the reality that those survivors who did make it to the Promised Land were then interned in camps like unwanted cattle.

SD: That's terrible....One more question. You say about how you're a Buddhist—from age eleven?—and it "outgrew the parent," and Christianity outgrew its parent....

BH: I'm impressed that you took notes! [She grins widely.] Simply, that Hinduism gave birth to Buddhism, and Judaism gave birth to Christianity and then Islam. So you have two religions which gave rise to three newer ones that became bigger—more populous—than their parent religions.

SD: Isn't it a shame they can't get along?

BH: Especially the three from western Asia. Now I'd like you to answer a question I was asked on TV last week.

SD: How did *you* answer it?

BH: You're the celebrity, I want to hear your opinion. The question: Why are there separate words—"gay" and "lesbian"—for homosexual men and women, when there's just one word for heterosexual men and women?

SD: Ow, that's so easy! Gays and lesbians don't go to bed together. Straights do. Is that what you said?

BH: I didn't get to—they went to commercials. That's what I would have said. Maybe in more words.

SD: Well, everyone forgets it's three groups, not two. It's two, politically: gays...and heterosexuals. But in regular life, it's three: men and women, men and men, and women with women.

BH: You should get a podium. This needs explaining.

SD: [Laughs.] Ow, you're just flattering me...or joshing me!

BH: No, but would you believe it if I told you that a classmate of mine in college was named Sandy Dennis and wore a lesbian button to school?

SD: [Shrieks.] *Ow!*...No. Really? No! It couldn't be; could it? Ow, you're pulling my leg....Is it *true*?

BH: Yes. *His* name was Sandy Dennis, and he wore one of those "Ronald Reagan is a Lesbian" buttons.

SD: Ow, I remember those! [Guffaws.] They must be worth a fortune now!

BH: You had them in New York? He was *our* governor.

SD: I don't think I ever saw one. But I *heard* about them, and I always wondered if he was going to sue....

BH: For being accused of lusting after women?

SD: [Whispering.] I heard something scandalous about one of his—[Stops.]

BH: **Kids?**

SD: No, wives....But we can't talk about it. You might do a Capote! [Laughs.] It's too bad. I *love* true gossip.

BH: **You want some?**

SD: What? Ow! *Tell* me.

BH: **Capote did me.**

SD: No! Really?! Ow!...Well,...after all...why not?

BH: **He claimed to have done Errol Flynn and countless others.**

SD: Was it...after you interviewed Truman?

BH: **Yes. It wasn't on the first interview.**

SD: Ow, my God! So, like, he gave you an earful, and you gave him a mouthful? [Grinning.]

BH: **You're leering....And you don't want to embarrass me.**

SD: I don't?

BH: **I'm not trying to embarrass you. This really is the next question on my list. See? [She looks, nods.] What does it do to a performer when a vicious critic like John Simon mauls an actress in print, cutting down what he imagines to be her physical shortcomings?**

SD: ...Um...you want to kill him. A natural instinct....It's so...vicious, he does it to actresses, not to men. To...well, Liza Minnelli and Streisand and me and....Ow, he said awful things about Brenda Vaccaro—to him, the worst thing he could say about her, in *Midnight Cowboy*, was she reminded him of a dyke. I mean a *dyke*! And he said it in *those* days! My God!

BH: **I think the reason he's cut back is because it's less acceptable now for him to spew such sexist and/or homophobic crap.**

SD: Please don't mention his name while we eat.

BH: **Okay. So first you want to murder him. Then what?**

SD: ...Then I burst out laughing. Probably.

BH: **Couldn't you do like Sylvia Miles and pour food on him?**

SD: Ow, I wish I could, but I just couldn't.

BH: **Too much the lady?**

SD: No, a coward! And a bad aim—I'd probably miss! [Shakes head.] Anyway, after what he wrote about me—things like, words like, whatever it was, and "still-born calf" and "nasal catarrh"—I just...I couldn't face him in person.

BH: **After all these years?**

SD: I have a *memory*. [Crossly.]

BH: **...What actress do you most admire?**

SD: [Puts finger to lips, shakes head.]

BH: **Least admire?**

SD: Mel Gibson. Ow, he's horrible! As a man. As a star, he's okay.

BH: **So long as he says someone else's lines? [She nods.] Who is the most masculine actress you know of?**

SD: My God, what a question! Ow....It was Lucille Ball. When she got really, really old. The voice dropped—the cigarettes and whatever—and she....God, was she bossy! She treated her husband [Gary Morton] like a servant. She bitched about everything, she just had to be in control.

BH: **You seem the opposite of a controller.**

SD: Ow, I just *give* it away...in some things. I don't need control. It's a big headache.

BH: **What sort of actress or woman do you not admire?**

SD: [Giggles.] Ow, you know—the kind who's so pampered and picky-picky, the kind that thinks she'll get athlete's foot from the sand, walking on the beach.

BH: A diva?

SD: No, I love divas. To watch, not to be near.

BH: I get the feeling that wardrobe isn't that important to you. I mean that kindly.

SD: No [holds out her hand and grabs my fingers, then releases them and pushes back her hair], I know you do. I know that....They're not—*clothes*. I like...clothes I don't have to notice.

BH: I like weather you don't notice.

SD: This coast, you *notice*.

BH: You went to school together, so did you know Dick Cavett well?

SD: Ow, not intimately! People want that, when they find out....Slightly, not intimately. I don't think anyone knows him intimately.

BH: That's what some people say about you....

SD: Ow! Stop that! [Giggles.] They have nasty minds, that's all!

BH: Nasty minds that don't believe your mind is at all nasty...?

SD: Believe me, I can...I get...I can have nasty thoughts.... I've been around.

BH: Around who?

SD: Never you mind! [Nods.] Never you mind.

BH: What do you think of female singers who come out?

SD: God bless 'em. Ow, absolutely....And they have the whole thing ahead of them.

BH: A good beginning makes for a good ending.

SD: Well, now...they can start at the beginning now....

BH: You mean come out of the closet young?

SD: Yes...yes, in their twenties. That's the time to do it.

BH: What about the saying, better late than never?

SD: That's good, too. For whoever.

BH: What women—not actresses—do you admire?

SD: Ow, lots and lots of women. But...I read this article in a magazine...a few years ago. It had a yucky title—"Golden Girls." Like the TV show. But it was about Emma Goldman and Golda Meir. Great women, both Jewish, and they had "gold" in their names.

BH: One wonders which came first? The article or the title?

SD: [Giggles.] "Golden Girls" is awful anyway. But I saw this wonderful title—I don't know if it's a poem or a story or a song or what it was, but I loved it. It was "Maria Callas's Lillies."

BH: A gardening book for opera lovers?

SD: ...I love animals, and they'll ask me about cats, and I love anything to do with cats. But you know what other animal I love?

BH: Catfish? Dogfish?

SD: No, but you're very warm...very *wet*. Seahorses!

BH: Seahorses? Why?

SD: You must not know about them....

BH: I don't even know why they call them seahorses.

SD: [Eagerly.] Did you know a seahorse is the only animal where the male carries the pregnancy? I'm not sure if a seahorse is really a fish, but I know, and I've read it more than once though I've never seen it on TV, that the female inserts her sort of nipple into the male and releases her eggs into his stomach. And they stay there....

BH: Gee. But why isn't her nipple-like thing then a penis, and why isn't she considered a he?

SD: Well, if you want terminology! [Laughs.]

BH: Isn't there any sperm involved? Presumably from the male?

SD: Well, that's why he's the male: after she puts her eggs in him, his sperm goes over the eggs and...whatever.

Fertilizes them, I think. Later, he gives birth to the baby seahorses—in the sea. He sort of discharges them.

BH: **Or emits them.**

SD: That's right. You can check all this out at your library.

BH: **You make a wonderful public service announcement.**

SD: [Laughs.] But it would be wonderful for people, if we had a choice! Barbara Walters asks people what kind of tree they'd want to be, but I'd never want to be a tree— they can't move or talk. And I've been asked what kind of animal I'd want to be, if I could come back as one, and I always said a cat. A house cat. In a nice house. But ever since finding out about seahorses...well, I'd have to change my answer.

BH: **Because you could get a male pregnant?**

SD: Well, yes. If you did want children, though one at a time, I mean as a female, I wouldn't have to be pregnant.

BH: **As Gloria Steinem says, if men got pregnant, abortion would be an enshrined right.**

SD: That's right. [Giggles.] No wonder we've never seen a Disney or a PBS documentary on the reproductive life of the seahorse!

BH: **Nature's too varied for television.**

SD: Human nature, too [nods]. They show the parts of nature they're comfortable with.

BH: **Speaking of pregnancies, what was the point in*Virginia Woolf*—we're back to your brilliant career, and it *is*—of your character having "hysterical pregnancies"?**

SD: Ow...that's so...I should ask Edward Albee. *You* should. That's so long ago.

BH: **Did you—like that homophobic critic—ever feel that Albee had meant George and Martha to be a male couple?**

SD: No one did! No one who was in it, or Edward, no... That's just whatever-his-name-was, he didn't want anyone to think there's ever been a straight couple that fights a lot.

BH: **I think he was also a hetero critic—not very straight in his logic—who resented a gay playwright's success.**

SD: And...anyway, heterosexuals have written most of the gay roles. Till recently.

BH: **And most of the female characters, and Oriental, Hispanic, etc., etc., have been written—usually unsympathetically—by white male heterosexuals.**

SD: Ow, yes. It's crazy....[Yawns.] Excuse me...tired. Why do you think when lesbians get middle-aged, they most of 'em get fat or dress in men's clothes?

BH: **"They"? [She giggles, puts her fingers to her lips.] Do you think there's such a thing as men's clothes anymore? Haven't men's clothes become everyone's clothes?**

SD: Yes...and I should have worn pants. I dunno. They can be too tight. It's embarrassing. A dress is...more billowy.

BH: **...I just want to say, your teacher was so moving, the kind of teacher we'd all like to have had in high school, in *Up the Down Staircase*. Your other most famous starring role was also in 1967, *The Fox*, from the D. H. Lawrence novella. Were you advised not to play lesbian?**

SD: Some...it was...I'd won an Oscar, so, you know, "You can play anything. You can get away with it." But some people did say I needed to watch out, and either get married and play a lesbian or stay single but don't play her. But after all, it was D. H. Lawrence, so it was...you know.

BH: **Literature? [She nods.] Before or after *The Fox*, was there much pressure on you to wed for your image?**

SD: They almost drove me to Valium, that's all!

BH: **Valium? That's too bad....I always thought a good title for a book on lesbian actresses could be *Violets and Valium*.**

SD: Why violets?

BH: The first successful lesbian-themed play on Broadway, in the 1920s, was *The Captive*. The lead character would send her female loves bouquets of violets.

SD: Ow, I remember! *Hearing* about it. The violets, a bunch of violets, it became like a...a symbol or...?

BH: A coded gesture. If a woman gave another violets, it meant she was expressing her interest.

SD: Ow, I wonder if I've given any ladies any violets over the years that I wasn't interested in like that, and they thought...? Ow, my God!

BH: Don't worry. Few people know about the violets.

SD: Sex and violets. Or, in order, violets, then sex.

BH: Hmm. Back to your lesbian role.

SD: Has Lily Tomlin ever played a lesbian?

BH: What brought that up?

SD: Well, I have. Why hasn't she? On the screen. Everyone's done it on the stage...I think.

BH: ...You're right. On the screen, she hasn't. It said somewhere, in some column, that she's declined a few lesbian roles.

SD: [Guffaws.] 'Nough of that. Back to me. Did you know that my lover's name—Anne Heywood, my lover in *The Fox*—her real name, she's English, is Violet Pretty? That's her real name! If we'd used it in the movie, even if they said it was by D. H. Lawrence, everyone would have said it was an unbelievable name.

BH: Violet Pretty? Amazing. Were you at all attracted to her, for real?

SD: Yes! I'm not going to lie...now. I've been asked that. They asked Susan Saran [Sarandon], and she said it was *wonderful* doing a love scene with Catherine Deneuve.

BH: I remember. She even said it in *Cosmopolitan*. No actor can admit that about another male actor.

SD: Well, in really ancient times, before the Greeks and Jews and everyone, women had the sexual power. It was part of the religion. Goddess worship, I think they call it.

BH: **I read a very informative book about that, by a woman named Merlin—Merlin Stone—called *When God Was a Woman*.**

SD: Ow, I should read that! I heard of it. But, getting back, it's...actresses play sex objects, so we can explore all the different sexualities, in different characters. That's a powerful thing, and men aren't allowed to do that.

BH: **Not more than one role, and not admitting they liked it.**

SD: *The Fox* was *not* stereotypical, was it?

BH: **No, it had texture and it subverted some of the stereotypes. But the ending is not Lawrence's ending, and it's the biggest reason it's considered an anti-lesbian film overall.**

SD: [Giggling.] Imagine having a tree fall between one's legs!

BH: **Heavy Freudian symbolism. She rejects the man between her legs, so she gets something far bigger, and fatal.**

SD: And she loses her girlfriend to a man.

BH: **It was the sixties, and lesbian characters always were won by men or they were killed off.**

SD: Even Pussy Galore in *Goldfinger*. Ow, I loved that name!

BH: **Yet it's a very interesting film.**

SD: *The Fox*? It is. The two women, they are. The man's just shallow. I mean as written. I sort of felt Anne could leave me for Keir [Dullea], she could experiment by having a sex-like affair with him, then come back to me. But they shouldn't have killed me off! [Shakes head.]

BH: **No, it's a very negative message about a lesbian woman who is lesbian and remains lesbian. A "sex--like" affair? [She nods and giggles.] Wonderful phrase....Have you had sex-like affairs?**

SD: With men or women?

BH: Women or men.

SD: Uh...Yes. Sex-like affairs, for me, are the best kind. Were the best kind. I think by now you know that I'm retired from sexual competition.

BH: You alluded to that, once.

SD: I'll be honest with you, it's...better.

BH: A relief?

SD: [Slowly.] I...never liked penetration. [Stares.]

BH: Who would? Although...with a man and a woman, it's sort of inevitable. [No reaction.] Unless it's oral...?

SD: There's what I mentioned with women, too....Enough about that, though....I was asked this terrifically intimate question once by this lesbian columnist, and...

BH: *The* gossip columnist?

SD: Yes...everyone knows. It really got my goat, 'cause she expected me to answer this...this....

BH: A question about being lesbian or bi?

SD: Yes! Very personal and for possible use in her column. I mean, who is she to ask me this and expect me to *tell* her, and...when she's always denying it herself, even though, I mean, she lives with....It's...augh!

BH: I know what you mean. You know, it's natural for sex to dwindle with the decades—to some degree—but what about the way an actor, as she gets older and more talented—more sure of herself, with more to give to audiences—gets less and less work? Fewer parts.

SD: Fewer and smaller, and that's where the damned ego thing comes in! Perhaps I shouldn't complain at all, I dunno. I went from supporting roles to...into the...being the main event, and then to supporting roles again. But I became *known*. Famous, maybe. I'm still famous in New York. But they'll offer me...a *nothing* role, and they seriously expect me to take it. I should be grateful, right? [Angry, hurt.] They don't respect the feelings of older ac—no, of older *women*. They don't care. Or care enough.

BH: **The way most of us take our mothers for granted?**

SD: Well,...if I hadn't gone from supporting to...something bigger, it wouldn't be like this. I could work more. But by doing less. One does get spoiled. You star in something, you at least expect medium-sized roles, afterwards. Something worth getting out of bed for.

BH: **Something exciting and big enough to maintain a healthy ego.**

SD: [Sighs.] But anyway. It's a tiresome...one gets tired. [Perks up.] I do my best! Here's that famous toothy smile again. [Laughs.] But if I had a daughter—not that I want one—*if* I had one, I wouldn't want her to be an actress.

BH: **How about an actor?**

SD: When and if...everyone, male and female actors, actresses and actors—whatever—are treated equally...equally well, and get the same respect and...opportunities, young or old, then all right! I'd say, "Go be an actor, dear. But don't get your hopes up."

BH: **I think that's a good place to end our public conversation. As usual, it's been nothing but a pleasure talking with you, Sandy.**

SD: Ow, Boze....I know. I know. Even though we're not saying goodbye now, I'd get up and hug you, but my foot's asleep! Ooh, it's like a dead weight. Ow, my God, how awful. I'll just sit very still.

BH: **It'll go away. Everything bad does.**

SD: Yeah! Everything good, too.

EPILOGUE

Ten lesbian or bisexual Hollywood women. Individuals on both sides of the camera, performers donning masks of comedy and/or tragedy. Most also choosing the public mask of sexual and affectional conformity.

Only Patsy Kelly, the most straightforwardly comedic of the group, was open about her minority status. None of the women, including Kelly, formally came out. Not in retirement, old age or after her career was long, long past, as with the famously sapphic Dorothy Arzner.

This has much to do with their generations and the eras they continued to live in. Three were born in the 1800s, only three were born since World War I, *all* before World War II. The next most open was Capucine, a Frenchwoman —one of the two non-Americans in the collection, with Australian-born British subject Judith Anderson.

Most of the conversationalists were typical of non-hetero-sexual women who achieved (is "overachieving" possible any-more?), in that they contractually wed. Four married as often as twice—low for Hollywood. Ironic, said Capucine, that affluent and ambitious lesbians seek matrimony more often than "similar women who are poorer or live in smaller towns where blending in is more necessary than in Paris, New York, or Hollywood." Most of these females agreed that women in show business are heavily pressured to get a man.

Arzner, the least conventionally feminine of the lot, could barely put up with her male bosses' demands and interference. Sandy Dennis wasn't prepared to put up with "that big draw-back to average men's company," their sexual demands, while Patsy freely admitted, "I like men, but not touching me. Unless it's a pat on the back—the *upper* back."

Yet if most tied a marital knot along the way, these ten weren't representative of hetero-, homo-, or bisexual women in another way. *None* bore a child. Actresses past and present tend to have considerably fewer offspring than non-entertain-ers. But a random sampling of ten lesbians or bisexual women in or out of show business would find that from one-third to two-thirds have borne or adopted one or more children.

Two actresses—the old-fashioned, twice-wed, and very serious Barbara Stanwyck and Agnes Moorehead—adopted. Each chose one child, a son. In one case, mother and son became permanently estranged, in the other, the son report-edly vanished. Is it significant that two such male-defined and closeted performers chose a son, not a daughter?

A few patterns emerged from my conversations. The comedic actors were generally more casual, less walled-in than their dramatic counterparts—excepting the youngest partici-pant, Sandy Dennis (adept at drama or comedy) and the Continental one. Oddly, the two women who worked behind the camera and thus had less "need" to stay in the closet, were among the most reticent. Arzner and Edith Head were genuinely shy personalities and both born in the Victorian era.

Each woman was an unforgettable encounter—including Ms. Arzner, the only one I didn't get to meet in person. With a few, once was enough. Stanwyck was hardened almost to the point of petrification. Anderson, Head, and Moorehead were brittle but less granite-like. Marjorie Main, Patsy Kelly, Nancy Kulp, Capucine, and Sandy Dennis were each a distinct pleasure, eventually feeling to me more like favorite aunts or elder sisters than interviewees.

As to why a lesbian subject is usually less forthcoming with a male interviewer than a gay subject, there are two basic reasons: a lesbian isn't sexually attracted to and may be wary of a male, whatever his age (as opposed to a somewhat or much older gay man or a bisexual woman); and the fact that women like our ten endure discrimination not only as non-heterosexuals but also because of their gender.

Still and all, I feel that this worthy and accessible group of individuals has shed more than a little light on that "other" half of the Hollywood closet.

INDEX